FOR PETE'S SAKE
The Influence of Pete Seeger

DOUG McPHILLIPS

Also, by Doug McPhillips:
Other Visionary Stories:
NOVELS.
From Darkness to Light.
Awake to my Gutted Dream.
The Sword of Discernment.
Santiago Traveller.
I Prophet.
Master's at my table.
The Guru of Jerusalem.
We are upside down. (Biography)
The Wicklow Way.
The Adventures of Ace McDice.
Instant Karma & Grace.
The Credo.
Reflections of an Old Man.
Reincarnation of the Assassin
Masters of Introspection.
Journey to a hermit's haven.
The Rise and Rise of a 4th Reich
Grandad's tales are tall and true.
Into Action: Alcoholics for Jesus
Lightbulb Moments
A Camino Guide Book.
Country Camino. (Album).
Santiago Traveller. (Album).
Soul Fact. (Album).

Apart from any fair dealing for private study, research, criticism or review, as permitted under the Copyright Act, no part may be reproduced by any process without the editor's written permission.
Doug McPhillips Circa 2025 ISBN. 978-1-763698390
National Library of Australia Catalogue-in-Publication data: New Holy Bible, International Version, Hodder & Stoughton, 1980.
Alcoholics Anonymous, 4th Edition, AA World Service, 1976.
As Bill sees it, 8th Print, AA World Service. 2017
Daily Reflections, 11th Print, AA World Service 2014.
Journey to the Inner Mountain, Hodder & Staughton, James Cowan, 2002.
The Choice is always ours, Jove Publishing, 1997.
Santiago traveller, Ingram Spark, Doug McPhillips, 2018.
Chopping Wood, Short Run Press, David Bernz, 2023
Where have all the flowers gone? WW Norton & Co, 2006
How to play a string banjo. Peter Seeger, self-published,1962
The Times and Times of Bob Dylan: A Biography. Lulu Press, 2016.
Woody Guthrie- A Life- Joe Klein, Random House, 1999
Notebook Research.
Google research- Authors Unknown.

This book blends fact and fiction. All characters in this novel are either factual or fictional, and the names of people living at the time may be real or imagined. Any resemblance to actual events, locales, or persons, living or dead, is purely coincidental; however, what is applicable is indeed real. Where poetic license transforms fact into fiction, names have been altered to protect the innocent.

For Lovers of Folk Music

And

Folk Heroes.

Introduction.

My earliest memories of Pete Seeger date back to a time of great sadness in my life. I vividly recall standing in the front garden of my parents' home at sunset on a dreary Saturday, just after witnessing the death of my blood brother John the week before. I was a sad, lonely, and blue boy, unsure of how to cope with this deep grief. Lost in the moment, I soon heard the sound of singing as a bus rumbled around the corner, passing by with a load of footballers returning from a match, singing in chorus, "Irene Goodnight." It wasn't the first time I had heard the song; it was a hit on the radio, a version of the 1931 recording by Huddie "Lead Belly" Ledbetter, later popularised by the folk music group The Weavers in 1949. It was the musical genius of Pete Seeger's banjo melody, combined with the unifying voices in the song's lyrics, that made it a sing-along favourite for the listening public. To me, it became a hallmark of what would come to define the Pete Seeger style.

It was the folksinger and his banjo melodies that drew me to Pete's songs. I was born in the age of the gramophone, listening to music on the local radio station. The bandwidth of the radio waves limited our listening to local commercial stations and the ABC. Additionally, we had the jukebox at our local Greek café, as well as what we picked up from the silver screen at the Saturday afternoon flicks. It was the 1950s, and Pete Seeger and The Weavers, apart from "Goodnight, Irene," enjoyed notable success with several songs, including "If I Had a Hammer (The Hammer Song)" and "We Shall Overcome."

By the time I reached my teens, Elvis Presley was all the rage, and like so many young teens, I was captivated by his music. The folk era had somewhat faded in Australia, while in the USA, many folk singers, like Pete Seeger, were being ostracised as communists, anti-American. It was a time of post-World War II nationwide anti-radical hysteria stirred by a growing fear that a Bolshevik revolution in America was imminent. This revolution would alter the church, home, marriage, civility, and the American way of life. Senator Joe McCarthy shot to public attention in 1950 with his claims that hundreds of Communists had infiltrated the State Department and other federal agencies. These accusations struck an exceptionally responsive chord during a time of intensifying national anxiety about the spread of world communism. Movie actors, producers, and those in the music industry were sidelined and struggled to find work. At that time, the Weavers disbanded because their music could not be played on the radio or shown on the new medium of TV.

We kids of the 1950s and 1960s were swept up in the era of Elvis and his films, which centred around romantic love, teenage rebellion, and musical performances. These movies often showcased Elvis as a charismatic, fun-loving character who used music to win over a love interest's affections and occasionally battled against villains. Many of these films also featured exotic locations and followed a familiar formula of songs, romance, and escapades. Additionally, the influence of James Dean's anti-establishment persona was starting to rub off on me. It wasn't long before my mates and I began emulating his actions and playing risky games of chicken.

Pete Seeger and folk music seemed to fade until the hit song "Where Have All the Flowers Gone?" came on the radio. Inspired by traditional folk songs he had encountered during a flight amidst the McCarthy era, Pete Seeger found a playlist of 60 anti-war songs, and the message of a peace song resonated with him. It was "Where Have All the Flowers Gone?", a song of peace, not war, that complemented both his state of mind and mine at the time. By then, I had become more involved in the peace movement, and folk music had regained its vogue for me. Besides, singers like Bob Dylan, Phil Ochs, and Johnny Cash suited my tastes more than the popular, clean-cut images that were available locally. Although I was also captivated by early Beatlemania, like most youths of the day, folk music took precedence over anything else. Message music ballads were more to my liking. By my early 20s, I was learning to stand on my own; the hard-drinking, smoking, and poetic bohemian style seemed to fit my persona in the early 1960s.

Meanwhile, Pete Seeger, labelled a communist, a non-establishment figure, and a civil rights radical, struggled to find consistent work. For many years, he made a living singing and teaching banjo to schoolchildren. Eventually, the idea of travelling the world with his family to perform concerts became his mission. Thus, in 1963, Pete Seeger emerged as one of the earliest supporters of Bob Dylan, playing a crucial role in encouraging A&R man John Hammond to produce Dylan's first album for Columbia and inviting him to perform at the Newport Folk Festival, where Seeger served as a board member.

I saw Pete Seeger perform in 1963 at the Sydney Town Hall, but he didn't "sink" or die there. He was a well-known folk singer and activist at the time, touring extensively worldwide, which included a one-night concert in Sydney and Melbourne that year. He was particularly recognised for his anti-war song "Waist Deep in the

Big Muddy," which he performed at the 1968 venue on his return to the stage in Sydney. I was by then captivated by concerts of Peter, Paul and Mary, who sang many of Pete Seeger's hits, including the popular Hammer song and later the Byrds' rendition of "Turn, Turn, Turn."

This work is not merely an autobiographical journey into Pete Seeger's life; it is also a chronicle of his influence on other musicians and songs from an era when I was young and impressionable. It's not intended to be an in-depth exploration of Pete Seeger or any of the musical geniuses who followed his style or path. Many authors are far more skilled in musicology, investigating the lives, careers, and artistic processes than I am. It aims to provide an account of the era and the mood that emerged when the Western world began shifting to a more radical perspective, as those who could foresee and express this shift through their music, politics, environmental views, and vocal opinions on civil rights. There was none as expressive in song and action in this regard as Pete Seeger. So I trust that you, the reader, may gain some insight into what was achieved by living in an era where icons of stage and screen contributed more to the standard of non-conformity than any political rally or contrarian viewpoint ever could. To a significant extent, the perspectives of such radical viewpoints, accompanied by a questioning mentality, resonated more with our generation than the indoctrination prevalent today. It is the lessons learnt from looking back and the promise of tomorrow that can only happen for human benefit if more independent souls like Pete Seeger rise to voice their opinions in song, in deed, and for the good of all concerned.

CHAPTER 1.

A SYNOPSIS OF THE SEEGERS.

Search for the name Pete Seeger on any search engine, and you'll find a summary of his achievements as a folk singer, songwriter, musician, teacher, conservationist, social activist, peacemaker, civil rights advocate, and devoted supporter of left-wing causes. In writing this opening chapter, I aim to set a template for what the book is about. It will offer you insight into what will follow, although not necessarily in chronological order. As I mentioned in the introduction, this narrative reflects both the influences Pete had on my life and my journey, as well as Pete's lifetime of achievements.

Pete Seeger was born on 3 May 1919 in New York's French Hospital to parents Charles and Constance Seeger. In his early adult life, Charles was a classical musicologist, composer, teacher, and folklorist. His first wife was Constance de Clyver Edson, a classical violinist and teacher; they divorced in 1927. They had three sons: Charles III (1912–2002), an astronomer; John (1914–2010), an educator; and Pete (1919–2014), who would later become known as an activist and folk singer. His second wife was the composer and musician Ruth Crawford Seeger (née Ruth Porter Crawford). Together, they had four children: Mike (1933–2009), Peggy (born 1935), Penny Seeger (1943-1993) and Barbara Seeger (1936-2025).

It was during a camping trip in 1921 that Charles and Constance conceived the idea of a travelling music roadshow, living a life akin to that of gypsies to bring classical music to the rural folk of America. However, the idea turned out to be unsuccessful, as they soon realised that the country folk had their musical roots deeply anchored in local storytelling, European ballads, African-American traditions, and a mix of indigenous influences. For Charles' brother Alan Seeger, fighting for the Allies was a moral imperative; in his poem "A Message to America," he spoke out against what he saw as America's moral failure to join the war. During the two years he spent fighting in the French Foreign Legion, Alan Seeger regularly wrote dispatches to The New York Sun. The essay "As a Soldier Thinks of War," published in Walter Lippmann's fledgling magazine, *The New Republic,* argued that although war was lamentable, it was also necessary. This cause of death was seen as inevitable and required. For the most part, his poetry from that time was not well known and did not gain recognition until after his death. As the war progressed, the theme of death grew stronger in his poetry, culminating in what became his most famous poem, "I Have a Rendezvous with Death."

Charles Seeger, like Pete's mother Constance, had music in his veins. Charles' family moved from Mexico City to New York in the late 1890s. Charles went on to graduate from Harvard in 1908, then studied in Cologne, Germany, and worked with the Cologne Opera. He left Germany to take a position as a Professor of Music at the University of California, Berkeley, where he taught from 1912 to 1916 before being dismissed for his public opposition to the USA's entry into World War I. One may well see that Pete's radicalism and musical inclination began with his early upbringing. However, it was undoubtedly the introspective poems of his Uncle Alan Seeger that most inspired Pete. Alan Seeger (22 June 1888 – 4 July 1916) was an American war poet who fought and died in World War I during the Battle of the Somme, serving in the French

Foreign Legion. Upon graduating from Harvard, Alan Seeger returned to Manhattan, primarily living in a boarding house at 61 Washington Square South, which became known variously as The Alan Seeger House or House of Genius. After two years, Seeger left Greenwich Village for Paris, where he resided in the Latin Quarter and continued to embrace a bohemian lifestyle.

In 1914, while living on Rue du Sommerard in Paris, war was declared between France and Germany. He quickly volunteered to fight as a member of the Foreign Legion, expressing that he was motivated by his love for France and his belief in the Allies' cause. His fellow legionnaire, Rif Baer, later described his last moments: "His tall silhouette stood out on the green of the cornfield. He was the tallest man in his section. With his head held high and pride in his eye, I saw him running forward, with bayonet fixed. Soon he disappeared, and that was the last time I saw my friend." Not only was Pete influenced by his uncle's poetic genius, but also by his views on leftist policies, which no doubt rubbed off on his nephew.

Charles Seeger, Pete's father, having learned lessons from the university of hard knocks during and after the war, turned to teaching at the Institute of Musical Art in New York from 1921 to 1933 and at the New School for Social Research from 1931 to 1935. Among Seeger's many specific interests were prescriptive and descriptive music writing, as well as determining the definition of what is meant by single style. In 1936, he was in Washington, D.C., serving as a technical advisor to the Music Unit of the Special Skills Division of the Resettlement Administration, which later became the Farm Security Administration. From 1957 to 1961, he taught at the University of California, Los Angeles. From

1961 to 1971, he served as a research professor at the Institute of Ethnomusicology at the University of California, Los Angeles (UCLA). In 1949–50, he served as a visiting professor of music theory at Yale University's School of Music. From 1935 to 1953, he held positions in the federal government's Resettlement Administration, Works Projects Administration, and Pan American Union, including serving as an administrator for the WPA's Federal Music Project, for which his wife also worked from 1938 to 1940. Charles's second wife, Crawford Seeger, returned to composition in 1952 with her Suite for Wind Quintet. By the time the composition was completed, Crawford Seeger had learned she had cancer and died in 1953. Charles passed away on February 7th, 1979, in Bridgewater, Connecticut. He was buried at Springfield Cemetery in Springfield, alongside his second wife. Charles established the first musicology curriculum in the United States at the University of California, Berkeley, during the 1910s. He also played a significant role in organising the American Musicological Society and was a key founder of the academic field of ethnomusicology.

In 1940, a year before Bob Dylan was born, Pete Seeger took the stage at the Forrest Theatre in New York alongside Woody Guthrie, the defining figure of American folk music in the 20th century. The occasion served as a benefit for migrant workers, but in retrospect, it proved to be a moment rich in cultural symbolism. 'Go back to that night when Pete first met Woody,' the American folk archivist Alan Lomax later told a journalist. 'You can date the renaissance of American folk song from that night.' Twenty-five years later, Pete Seeger was also backstage when Bob Dylan, the other defining figure of American folk music, led his electric band out to face the audience at the Newport Folk Festival and single-handedly ended that same folk renaissance. Dylan's subsequent performance has attained the status of myth. A significant part of that myth is that Seeger, one of the festival's organisers, was so incensed by Dylan's amplified assault on the audience that he attempted to sever the band's instrument cables with an axe. It's a great story, but not entirely true. In the heat of the moment, Seeger had indeed wished aloud for an axe, but only, he said later, because the noise of the band was drowning out the political message of 'Maggie's Farm'. Pete had taken his ageing father to the concert, and he wanted his dad to appreciate the meaning behind Dylan's song lyrics.

What is undoubtedly true is that Seeger saw Dylan's performance as nothing less than a betrayal of all that the festival organisers held: that folk music was essentially acoustic; that the folk song was a moment of intimate connection between performer and audience; that folk music was a medium for purveying a message and bolstering the essential solidarity that any left-leaning movement needed for its very survival—a betrayal, then, of folk itself. He must also have been offended by Dylan's attitude in turning the festival on its ear and turning his back on the one man who had backed him in his early career, namely the security and music contact at Columbia Records through a mutual friend, John Hammond, the producer at the time.

In that moment of impotent anger, Seeger's reputation shifted from pioneer to purist. The voice that had rung so many changes during the years between Woody Guthrie's reign and Dylan's turbulent ascendancy seemed suddenly and embarrassingly out of step amid the clamour of the new. To a degree, Pete Seeger has remained on the margins ever since, with his increasingly rare live appearances and records serving as a reminder for the faithful of how things used to be. Much of his isolationism may well have stemmed from his refusal to answer questions posed by the House Un-American Activities Committee (HUAC) during an investigation into suspected Communist infiltration in the entertainment industry back in 1957. Seeger's refusal to cooperate with HUAC and answer questions about his political beliefs and affiliations led to his indictment. He was convicted of contempt of Congress in 1961 and sentenced to a year in prison, but his conviction was later overturned on appeal. Despite his conviction being overturned, Seeger faced ongoing backlash and blocklisting, especially in the entertainment industry, for several years afterwards. He had to inform the government of his whereabouts whenever he left the Southern District of New York. Seeger's stance was grounded in his belief that the questions posed by HUAC violated his fundamental constitutional rights, particularly his right to freedom of speech. He argued that it was inappropriate for the government to inquire into his personal and political beliefs. While the initial focus was on his refusal to testify, Seeger's prior association with the Communist Party and his outspoken views on social and political issues also added to the controversy surrounding his case.

In the Fifties, amid the anti-communist hysteria stoked by Senator McCarthy, Seeger's concerts were frequently picketed, earning him the nickname 'Kruschev's Songbird'. In 1955, when he was summoned before the House Un-American Activities Committee and later indicted for contempt after asserting the Fifth Amendment, stating: 'I am not going to answer any questions as to my philosophical or religious beliefs, or my political beliefs ... or any of these private affairs.' Throughout this period, Seeger serves as a reminder of what has been gained and what has been lost. Ultimately, it may be Seeger's belief in the folk song as an agent of social change that becomes his enduring legacy, rather than the songs themselves. The essential dilemma at the heart of his calling lies here, showcasing his unwavering commitment.

In 1994, it was ironic that the man who had been feared as a communist sympathiser during the McCarthy witch hunt and who faced charges in his youth was honoured with the National Medal of the Arts at the age of 75. Upon presenting the award, President Bill Clinton described him as "an inconvenient artist, who dared to sing things as he saw them." Pete Seeger was a truly remarkable man. By the age of 85, Seeger lived in virtual seclusion in the woods near Beacon, New York, and one suspects he would have preferred to be out of the limelight without the media attention that the Springsteen album, dedicated to Pete Seeger songs, has brought back into the public's focus.

Looking back on his roots, we note that Pete was a Harvard graduate from a bourgeois background, while Seeger was an unlikely Marxist folk singer, being introspective and reserved. According to David Hajdu, in his study of the Sixties protest folk era, Positively 4th Street, Seeger took up performing as an act of virtue, believing from the outset that 'a song could change the world'. When Seeger teamed up with Guthrie in the Almanac Singers, it was as if a beacon was being passed from one generation to the next. Guthrie was only seven years older than Seeger but was of a different ilk; his songs were steeped in experience, reflecting the eternal outsider. As Hajdu memorably puts it, 'Pete Seeger embodied idealism; Woody Guthrie, realism.' That distinction is crucial in comprehending all that followed.

While Guthrie engaged in what Hajdu describes as 'poetic reportage', Seeger's best-known songs were 'political homilies'. Before Bob Dylan penned 'Blowin' in the Wind', Seeger's renditions of 'Where Have All the Flowers Gone' and 'We Shall Overcome' had become the rallying cries of a new kind of protest folk movement. However, that movement, as those now timid-sounding songs suggest, was essentially middle class. Most of its leaders, along with its audience, came, like Seeger, from comfortably well-off backgrounds.

For all that, though, Seeger was an activist who believed passionately in the power of song and the communal nature of performance. His best songs, such as 'If I Had a Hammer', often adhered either to the sing-along form or to the simplicity of children's rhymes.

In an era when even the finest contemporary American folk music is characterised by ironic detachment, it is also challenging to convey the kind of commitment demonstrated by performers like Seeger. In a recent New Yorker profile, he recalled a benefit for the Harlem Civil Rights Congress, which took place in 1949. The star was the great American singer and actor Paul Robeson. The Ku Klux Klan tore down the stage, and the concert was postponed. When it eventually occurred, Robeson had to perform with men standing around him on stage to prevent snipers from shooting him. The bus carrying Seeger, his wife, and young children passed mobs of raucous onlookers who spat and shouted obscenities, and, after the show, it was attacked by stone-throwing youths while police stood by and watched. Seeger has two of the rocks that crashed through the bus window embedded in his fireplace.

In 1950, however, as a member of the Weavers, Seeger became an unlikely pop star when their saccharine version of Leadbelly's 'Goodnight Irene' became the best-selling single of the year. Celebrity, however, was not his calling, and he retreated to the backwoods.

Many of Seeger's songs became trademarks of the various social movements that inspired his passion and fight. "Where Have All the Flowers Gone," one of his best-known songs, became a regular anthem in the anti-war movement of the 1960s and '70s. "We Shall Overcome," an early gospel song adapted by Seeger from "We Will Overcome," served as a rallying cry during the Civil Rights Movement of the 1960s. Pete Seeger, the legendary folk musician, recorded over 100 albums throughout his lifetime and influenced an extensive and impressive list of artists, including Bob Dylan, Joan Baez, Bruce Springsteen, Peter Yarrow of Peter, Paul and Mary, and Bernice Johnson Reagon of Sweet Honey in the Rock, to name just a few. Pete helped spearhead the American folk revival and passed away on Monday, 27th January 2014, in New York City at the age of 94 from natural causes. Across more than seven decades, he inspired countless singer-songwriters, activists, and social movements. Just before his death, he was serenaded in his hospital bed by close friends.

David Amram, a fellow musician and long-time friend of Seeger, was among the group who sang to him. "I was fortunate enough to be able to say goodbye to him during the last two hours of his life. As we played some music for him and his family in his hospital room, we could feel his spirit fill our hearts with that endless energy he shared with the world for 94 years," wrote Amram in an email to friends and family in Seeger's honour. "Ever since he chose his path, he has stayed on it and walked the walk he talked and inspired generations to raise our voices in song, to always think of others, to respect ourselves and all who cross our paths and to share whatever blessings we have with others."

The legacy of Pete Seeger.

Now, here is a story of Pete Seeger
A legendary American folksinger,
To us folk of the 60s, he was more than that;
He was a patriot, a pacifist, a freedom fighter,
And more than that;
For that is not all that made up the man,
He was against the war in Vietnam,

Marched for freedom and sang some songs
About cleaning up the Hudson River
And educating the young.

As Pete sang:
"And I'll keep on singing
and marching along,
'Ever Onward', I'll be marching
For a mission to win "Ever Onward."

"You may love me cause I'm a Liberal,
Cast me off as a commie spy,
I'll sing in court in your trial of mischief
For you, call me an anti-government guy."

But I'll keep singing on this peaceful day,
Keep on the course of the Clearwater Way.

CHAPTER 2.

THE FOLK BEACON

On July 14, 1912, singer-songwriter Woody Guthrie was born in Okemah, Oklahoma, to musically inclined parents, Nora Belle (Sherman) and Charles Guthrie. It's tough to categorise Guthrie, who rose to fame during the Great Depression as a champion of the dispossessed and downtrodden, in a single way. He was a poet, philosopher, political revolutionary, environmentalist, and an admirer of Jesus Christ who scorned organised religion. His life was marked by tragedy from an early age and continued to be so until the end. His sister fatally set herself on fire during an argument with their mother when he was 7, his father was severely burned in a house fire, and Woody's firstborn died at age 4 when she was burned in an electrical fire. His mother was committed to the Oklahoma Hospital for the insane when he was 14, while he unknowingly carried the Huntington's chorea gene that led to their deaths after lengthy hospitalisations.

Musically inclined like his parents, he dropped out of high school as a senior and began playing for dances with his uncle in Texas. He married Mary Jennings in 1931. They divorced in 1940. He married twice more, to Marjorie Greenblatt (1945–53) and Anneke Van Kirk (1953–56), with whom he fathered eight children.

He had headed to California in the Dust Bowl migration, leaving the family temporarily in Texas. He hosted a "hillbilly" music radio show, made friends with people like Will Geer and John Steinbeck and wrote a column titled "Woody Sez" for the communist newspaper People's World in 1939-40 but never joined the political party. He joined the U.S. Merchant Marine in 1943 and was drafted into the Army in 1945. He wrote patriotic songs backing the U.S. fight against fascism. Guthrie wrote what became "This Land Is Your Land," arguably his most famous song, in February 1940. Tired of hearing Kate Smith sing "God Bless America" on the radio, he sarcastically called his song "God Blessed America for Me" before renaming it when it was first recorded in 1944, when God was excised from the title and lyrics. As initially written, it said:

One bright sunny morning in the shadow of the steeple
by the Relief Office, I saw my people
as they stood hungry, and I stood there wondering if
God blessed America for me.

Guthrie wrote over 3,000 song lyrics, including fanciful ones for children, as well as songs that have influenced succeeding generations of musicians, most notably his son, Arlo. His first album, "Dust Bowl Ballads" (1941), sold more than any other. His songs took the side of the economic refugees and those beset by tragedy against the "interests" and bankers. A line in "Pretty Boy Floyd" sums it up: "Some will rob you with a six-gun / And some with a fountain pen." He also published two novels, created artworks and wrote numerous published and unpublished manuscripts, poems, prose and plays. Over 400 of his songs are in the Library of Congress.

In March 1940, Woody Guthrie was invited by Pete Seeger to join the Almanac Singers, a group of folk singers that included Millard Lampell and Lee Hays. Seeger had formed a band to play at a benefit hosted by the John Steinbeck Committee to Aid Farm Workers, which raised money for migrant workers. At that time,

Woody was travelling throughout the US and made his way to New York to join the singing group on the radio. Both Pete and Woody became good friends and shared a loft in Greenwich Village. Later, with little to do besides travel and sing songs for far-flung communities, Pete accompanied Woody back to Texas to meet other members of the Guthrie family.

Pete Seeger was a skilled banjo player influenced by Guthrie's message on his guitar, "This machine kills fascists," and later crafted a similar slogan for his banjo, "This machine surrounds hate and forces it to surrender." They travelled together, sharing songs and experiences, and Guthrie's influence on Seeger's musical style and activism was substantial. Guthrie shaped Seeger's musical style, and Seeger, in turn, helped make Guthrie's songs more approachable for a wider audience. While not always formal co-writes, they often collaborated on songs and arrangements.

Peter met Toshi Ohta, a young woman of Japanese descent. Toshi was raised in Greenwich Village and Woodstock, New York. She attended the Little Red School House in Manhattan and graduated from the High School of Music and Arts in 1940. She met Pete Seeger at a square dance in 1939, and they courted for three years before marrying in 1943. Pete brought their engagement ring, which he had borrowed money for from his grandmother.

Later, in 1949, they moved from Greenwich Village to a log cabin built by Pete at Beacon, about 60 miles from New York, overlooking the Hudson River. At the time, it was a basic existence with no running water or electricity. Toshi is credited with laying the foundation for Seeger's personal and professional success. Toshi, along with their children, accompanied Pete to his hearings before the House Un-American Activities

Committee in Washington during the 1950s. Pete was cited for contempt of Congress, but his conviction was later overturned in 1961.

At the time Pete and Toshi Seeker settled into their hillside cabin with 17 acres of land overlooking the Hudson River, Beacon had a population of about 10,000, still recovering from the post-World War II era and transitioning from a manufacturing town to a more tourist-oriented destination. The city was known for its role in manufacturing, particularly hats, and its proximity to the Hudson River. A notable event at the time the Seegers moved into their log cabin in 1947 was the unveiling of the first monument to the war dead in Beacon, marking the end of World War II.

The area near Beacon was inhabited by the Wappinger and Munsee Native American tribes before European colonisation. The Munsee lived on the opposite side of the river, coexisting with the Wappingers. This is evident in settlements like Fishkill Landing and Matteawan, which are now part of what is known as Wappinger territory, a section of the larger Mohawk Confederacy that occupied the area around Beacon. They lived a semi-nomadic lifestyle, practising agriculture and hunting, and their territory stretched across the Hudson River valley, including the regions around Fishkill Landing and Matteawan. The Dutch settled along the Hudson River, establishing the villages of Matteawan and Fishkill Landing in 1709. These villages were later incorporated into the city of Beacon in 1913.

While the land that would become Beacon was purchased from the Wappinger tribe in 1683, Native Americans continued to live in the area until white settlers began to encroach on their traditional hunting grounds. The Dutch, along with other Europeans, began settling in greater numbers in the area in the early 18th century, with Matteawan and Fishkill Landing forming the earliest communities in the region. The natives were forced into the hilly country away from the Hudson River, and ultimately, further land grabbing led to their being placed on reservations, particularly after the two World Wars of the 20th century.

In 1949, when Pete Seeger moved to Beacon, New York, it was a small, industrial city with a more rustic and less artsy vibe than it has today. The Hudson River was heavily polluted at the time, making it a "convenient sewer" in Seeger's words. Seeger chose to live on a hilltop on the edge of town, building a simple log cabin with his bare hands, without the comforts of modern amenities like running water or electricity.

Between the 1950s and 1970s, Beacon, New York, thrived as a manufacturing hub and a strong tourist draw, thanks in part to the Mount Beacon Incline Railway. Within the town boundary, there was a brick and hat factory, a file manufacturing plant, the first lawnmower factory in America, and a flour mill. These factories employed thousands, and the Mount Beacon incline railway was a major tourist attraction, featuring a hotel and casino that drew tourists from around the world. However, the decline of manufacturing in the late 1960s and 1970s led to economic downturn and a gradual decline in the city's Main Street. As factories closed and residents sought jobs elsewhere, the city's economy suffered, impacting Main Street and leaving many commercial spaces vacant. The Dutchess Ski area closed in 1975, and the factories shuttered, marking the end of Beacon's manufacturing heyday. The economic downturn lasted from roughly 1970 to the late 1990s, during which many commercial spaces and factories remained vacant.

Pete Seeger was a prominent figure in the Beacon community in its decline, particularly known for his environmental activism and musical contributions. He and his wife, Toshi, founded the Hudson River Sloop Clearwater in 1966, an organisation dedicated to protecting the Hudson River and its surrounding areas, and cleaning up the Hudson. They built the sloop Clearwater and organised the Great Hudson River Revival, a music and environmental festival. Seeger also played music at local events and was a regular presence at community celebrations, such as the Pumpkin Festival and the Spirit of Beacon Parade. He was a beloved figure in Beacon, known for his music, activism, and community involvement. He often played music at community events, including the Pumpkin Festival and the Spirit of Beacon Parade. He also led sing-alongs and music circles at the Beacon Sloop Club, encouraging community participation in music.

Pete Seeger was involved in various local initiatives, including supporting the local schools and participating in the Martin Luther King Jr. celebration. He was known for his ability to connect with people and foster a sense of community. In essence, Pete Seeger's impact on Beacon went beyond his fame as a musician. He became a symbol of community involvement and environmental stewardship, leaving a lasting legacy in the town.

When Pete Seeger's ban from television appearances due to his political views was lifted in 1965, Toshi produced and directed a TV series, Rainbow Quest, hosted by Pete from 1965 to 1966. Japanese actress Eriko Hatsune portrayed Toshi's role as producer and director in the 2024 film "A Complete Unknown," directed by James Mangold. Her official credited title for the show was "Chief Cook and Bottle Washer." Toshi and Pete Seeger co-founded both the Hudson River Sloop Clearwater and its musical offshoot, The Great Hudson River Revival, later known as the Clearwater Festival. She used the festival to rally public support for cleaning up the Hudson River. Under her direction, the festival also introduced several ideas that were not utilised at other music festivals during the 1970s and 1980s, including sign language interpreters, wheelchair-accessible facilities for people with disabilities, and recycling programs. She recruited up-and-coming musical artists to perform at the festival through its planning committee, including Tracy Chapman, before they achieved popularity elsewhere. The Clearwater Festival now attracts over 15,000 attendees to Croton Point Park each summer. Toshi Seeger was later the executive producer of the 2007 documentary, "Pete Seeger: The Power of a Song," which won an Emmy Award. She was 85 years old at the time the documentary was produced. She served on numerous civic, environmental, and artistic organisations, including the New York State Council of the Arts.

In the late 1960s, Pete Seeger's travels with his family, particularly his sailing on the Hudson River, were motivated by a desire to raise awareness about environmental issues, especially the pollution of the Hudson River, and to advocate for social change. He founded the Hudson River Sloop Clearwater, an organisation dedicated to protecting the river and its surrounding areas. He used the sloop Clearwater as a floating ambassador for his environmental message. He also believed that music could be a powerful tool for social movements, and his travels were an extension of this belief, fostering participation and a sense of community.

Pete Seeger identified as a pantheist and did not believe in organised religion. He believed in the interconnectedness of all things and viewed God as encompassing everything. While he drew inspiration from specific religious themes, such as social justice, he was not a traditional Christian believer, as he found aspects of the Bible to be disagreeable. Seeger's beliefs were shaped by his upbringing in a family with a strong religious background, but he eventually distanced himself from traditional religious beliefs. He was a member of a Unitarian Universalist church, primarily for practical reasons, such as having a rehearsal space for his music; however, he later adopted a pantheistic view of God. In summary, Seeger adopted a pantheistic understanding of God, believing that God is everything, while avoiding the doctrines of organised religion. He found inspiration in various religious themes, particularly those related to social justice, but he was not a conventional believer.

I attended a Pete Seeger concert in Sydney in 1963. In 1963, he was touring Australia as part of a 10-month world tour, having been blocked in the United States. Like my young friends at the time, I was undergoing a psychological and environmental shift, embracing all things radical and peace-oriented. I had just missed being called up to serve in the Vietnam War twelve months before. It had been a sigh of relief and, at the same time, a psychological difficulty for me, as I had been conditioned to adhere to the needs of our country, but not so much as applied to the youth of America, for we were but a minor player in world affairs. However, there I was with my best mate, John, at a Pete Seeger concert, just a short time before he was scheduled to fly out to fight in Vietnam.

Pete Seeger profoundly influenced us young people in the 1960s and beyond, becoming a symbol of protest and social change through his music and activism. He inspired a generation to embrace folk music and engage with social justice issues, particularly the Civil Rights movement and opposition to the Vietnam War. Pete Seeger's "Where Have All the Flowers Gone?" and other songs advocated for peace, social justice, and a hopeful future. He used his music to address anxieties about war, nuclear annihilation, and the need for unity and understanding, reflecting a broader theme of inspiring people to love one another and live up to their nation's ideals, popularising songs like "We Shall Overcome" and "If I Had a Hammer," which became anthems of the Civil Rights Movement and other social movements.

Seeger actively supported the Civil Rights Movement by performing at rallies and advocating for equality, which earned him the respect of many young people in Australia. Furthermore, Pete's staunch opposition to the Vietnam War resonated with young people who felt disillusioned by the conflict and the broader societal issues of the time. Meanwhile, he was committed to environmentalism, particularly his efforts to clean up the Hudson River, which further endeared him to a generation concerned about

environmental issues. He was also working tirelessly to mentor other young artists, such as Bob Dylan and Joan Baez, inspiring them and contributing to the broader folk music movement. Seeger showed that protest music could be both meaningful and lasting, inspiring future generations to use music as a means for social change.

Pete Seeger's involvement with the Civil Rights Movement, anti-Vietnam War protests, and leftist ideals had a significant impact on these social movements and the broader political landscape. His musical activism and advocacy helped raise awareness and galvanise support for these causes, ultimately contributing to the passage of the Civil Rights Act of 1964, the end of the draft, and increased public awareness of the war's consequences. Seeger's music and activism helped to raise public awareness about the war's brutality and the injustices of the draft. Pete Seeger's songs like " We Shall Overcome" resonated with the young of the Vietnam era and became an anthem for the Civil Rights movement, particularly in America. He played a key role in mobilising protesters, including the March on Washington in 1963, which drew over 250,000 people, inspiring hope and solidarity among activists. The anti-war movement ultimately led to the elimination of the draft.

Seeger's music and activism were deeply intertwined with the counterculture of the 1960s, a movement that challenged traditional values and institutions. He advocated for social justice and equality, aligning with broader leftist ideals that gained prominence during this period. The leftist movement, driven by activists like Seeger, had a lasting impact on American politics, resulting in reforms in areas such as civil rights, environmental protection, and social welfare. In Australia, the May 8, 1970, Vietnam Moratorium protests—the most significant public demonstrations in Australia's history at the time—were key events that contributed to a moratorium against the Vietnam War. These marches, which involved over 200,000 people across Australia, were fuelled by a rising opposition to the war and conscription. One of the new government's initial decisions in 1972 was to end national service.

Creations of the Heart.

In the mind's eye of a dreamer
It's a quest,
like an artist carving images
from stone,
Maybe there is nothing on
the other side,
Just some crumbling stone.

Still, the living can take shape.
In the mind of man,
Springs always take new forms
In a heart of stone,
Walking on this pathway,
On my way home.

In the mind's eye of the dreamer,
Life has meaning,
joins the artist, carving forms,
New life takes shape,
springs the twinkling of the stars,

In the dream, there is a reason,
for the stone's new shape.

Perhaps that's why the cowboy
rides the ranges,
burning eyes of coal
on the night's log fire,
walking on some lofty hill
at midnight,
seeking out the home
of his desire."

How shall we view
The Temple of Creation,
sense the obstacles dissolve,
In some sacrifice,
for the working of the mind
a crucifixion, on the dressed altar,
the mind's creative light.

Many are the instruments
of the searching,
The workings of the mind,
the body, soul, seeking out some magic
of the utterance,
n coloured painted clay,
In human stone.

Hear the strings pluck
Fingers at the chords,
sound vibrations,
cries the voice, a hammered tone,
primary dance of the body,
a movement of the human soul's state.

CHAPTER 3.

ALL ABOUT WOODY GUTHRIE

I had not realised until my later years just how much those protest songs about civic liberties, war, and peace had indoctrinated a way of thinking in me that has persisted throughout the majority of my life, from childhood onwards, through the early 1960s and early 1970s. Woody Guthrie's songs during the Depression and afterwards were written at a time when many Americans were grappling with poverty, unemployment, and hunger. Woody Guthrie and Pete Seeger, both prominent figures in American folk music, shared a passion for social justice and themes related to the working class. However, their styles and songwriting approaches differed. Guthrie's songs, such as "This Land Is Your Land," are known for their poetic reportage and realism, often documenting his own experiences as an outsider. In contrast, Seeger's songs, such as "If I Had a Hammer," are more akin to political homilies, expressing a more idealistic vision of change. While Guthrie's songs were rooted in the experiences of the working class, Seeger's were more focused on enacting positive change and social activism through music.

Guthrie's songs focused on the realities faced by the struggling American working class, particularly during the Dust Bowl drought and the Great Depression. His songwriting style was characterised by a blend of traditional folk elements with a poetic and reportorial approach. He employed simple melodies and memorable lyrics that encouraged sharing. Yet, the lyrics often reflected his deeply personal experiences. His songs frequently addressed themes of social inequality, injustice, and the struggles of migrant workers.

Guthrie's songs have been widely covered and interpreted by many artists, including Bob Dylan, who wrote "Song to Woody" as a tribute to him. Pete Seeger, on the other hand, crafted songs more explicitly focused on activism and social change, using his music to promote progressive political and social ideals. Seeger's songs were often simple in structure, yet he was renowned for their powerful and clear messages. His melodies were typically straightforward and easily singable, making them accessible to a broad audience. Essentially, Guthrie was a "realist" who documented the struggles of the working class, while Seeger was an "idealist" who used his music to advocate for positive social change. Both men played a profound role in shaping the American folk music tradition, but they approached their roles and messages in distinct ways.

Woody Guthrie hitchhiked his way across the country to California in 1940 to share his talent at a midnight benefit concert for migrant workers. It was there he met Pete Seeger. They struck up a lifelong friendship and sang and collaborated in a lyrical and musical style more central to leftist and communist ideals of the time. The concert had been organised by a well-known leftist actor, Will Geer, in a small theatre on Broadway, just a block from Times Square in New York City, which was the heart of the entertainment district. A film depicting the Depression era captivated the public's attention. The movie, 'The Grapes of Wrath', based on the novel by John Steinbeck, tells the story of the struggles faced by migrant workers during the Great Depression. It portrays the effects of the Dust Bowl on families who must travel to other parts of the country (California in the novel) and the challenges they encounter while trying to build a better life for themselves.

To a great extent, it parallels Woody's life story, except that his life and experiences during the same period were more harrowing. Woody's childhood also mirrored another film, with Will Geer in the lead role, called 'Tobacco Road'. It told of a low-income family in rural Georgia struggling to make ends meet, as the clan's father, Jester Lester, proudly refused help at every turn. Although the Lesters had thrived on their land for generations, Jester and his wife had not prospered, and the family's outlook was bleak.

In reality, Woody Guthrie was named after the man who would become the twenty-eighth president of the United States. Woodrow "Woody" Wilson Guthrie was born on July 14, 1912, in Oklahoma to Nora and Charley Guthrie. Woody was the third of the couple's five children, but Charley had no trouble supporting his growing family. His real estate business thrived, and he also dabbled in politics, being an active member of the KKK at the time. From the beginning, music was a part of Woody's life. Often, Charley and Nora would "sing apart and together on hymns, spiritual songs, songs about how to save your lost and homeless soul and self. The colour of the songs was the Red Man, the Black Man, and the White folks."

Along with music, as previously mentioned, tragedy also impacted his early years. When Woody was just a toddler, the Guthries' newly built home burned down before the family had a chance to move in. Then, in 1919, Woody's sister Clara tragically lost her life in a fire. For some time leading up to this disaster, Nora had been acting erratically. Afterwards, Woody noted, "My mother's nerves gave away like an overloaded bridge." She even experienced occasional violent episodes and may have accidentally set Charley on fire in 1927, a situation that led to a long and painful recovery for him and to her commitment to the state mental hospital in Norman. It turned out that Nora had Huntington's disease, a progressive neurological disorder that affects movement, cognition, and emotional health. Symptoms vary in severity and presentation, including involuntary jerking movements, cognitive difficulties, and mental health changes like depression and mood swings. It was that hereditary disease that eventually killed Woody, too.

Due to the combined hardships of the Great Depression and the drought, many people from Oklahoma, Texas, Arkansas, and Missouri packed their belongings and travelled west in search of work. An estimated 400,000 made their way to California. Already somewhat accustomed to rambling, and with good reason this time, Woody hoboed his way to Los Angeles in 1936, where he eventually formed a musical partnership with his cousin, Jack Guthrie. They performed country-western tunes around town and promoted themselves on radio station KFVD. Later, Jack took a break from show business for a while, and Woody began singing with Maxine Crissman's radio show, whom he dubbed "Lefty Lou." This pairing was so successful that he was able to bring Mary and their kids to Los Angeles in 1937. Many of the songs Woody and Lefty Lou performed were old-style tunes such as "A Picture from Life's Other Side" and "Boll Weevil." But Woody also began featuring some of his original compositions in their shows; among these, both "Talking Dustbowl Blues" and "Do Re Mi" explored and exposed the harsh reality of the California-as-promised-land myth.

Although perceptions of California as a land of unrestrained opportunity attracted a wave of agricultural workers from the South and Southwest in the mid-1930s, the reality was quite different. The vast farms that spread across California's fertile valleys required workers to pick their crops. However, with so many workers available, wages steadily decreased, even if a family managed to secure consistent employment harvesting the state's many seasonal crops. The pickers lived in their cars, tents, or shacks made from whatever materials they could find. These camps were sometimes called "Hoovervilles," and the people in them were often referred to as "Okies."

While Woody never lived in one of these camps, he travelled to California as a "Dust Bowl refugee." During the spring of 1938, he moved around the state, singing to the migrant labourers and often hopping on freight trains for free rides to his next destination. He also performed at government camps, providing these individuals with a degree of dignity, health, and safety. Accompanying him was Will Geer, the actor and committed left-winger, who helped Woody develop a deeper understanding of the injustices within an economic system that allowed people to live in such poverty.

Before these troubles hit the family, they had already endured difficult times. Charley lost his land holdings and a significant portion of his self-esteem during the oil boom that followed World War I in eastern Oklahoma. Although he held a series of jobs after this loss, none paid well, and the Guthries fell into poverty. When Charley left Okemah after his injury, he took the two younger children, Mary Jo and George, while Woody and his older brother Roy remained behind to fend for themselves.

In 1929, Woody joined Charley in Pampa, Texas, a town located in the panhandle region near Amarillo, where other family members also resided. Jeff Guthrie, Charley's half-brother, taught Woody how to play guitar after he moved there. Uncle Jeff was a talented musician who had even won some regional fiddling contests. Although they often played together for fun, Uncle Jeff's skill far exceeded Woody's. Instead, Woody found other beginner musicians to jam with and formed the Corncob Trio. One of the members was Matt Jennings, whose younger sister Mary caught Woody's eye. They married in 1933 and eventually had three children together.

Times continued to be tough for Woody. By the time of his marriage, many changes had come to the region. The Great Depression had already swept across the nation, and a drought hit the plains in the early 1930s. Over-ploughing had removed the natural prairie grasses, and the wind swept up the dry earth in great waves that could blot out the sun. One journalist who came to the area famously dubbed it "The Dust Bowl." In the mid-1930s, Woody first realised the power of music to capture the truth about people and places. In thinking back about this time, he wrote, "there on the Texas plains right in the dead center of the dust bowl, with the oil boom over and the wheat blowed out and the hard-working people just stumbling about, bothered with mortgages, debts, bills, sickness, worries of every blowing kind, I seen there was plenty to make up songs about." One of his first songs to reflect what he saw happening around him became one of his most famous, "So Long, It's Been Good to Know You."

Due to the combined hardships of the Great Depression and the drought, many people from Oklahoma, Texas, Arkansas, and

Missouri packed up their belongings and travelled west in search of work. An estimated 400,000 made their way to California.

When Geer left California for New York to play Jeeter Lester in *Tobacco Road*, he urged Woody to visit. A few months later, with opportunities in Los Angeles drying up, Woody moved his family back to Texas before relocating to New York City in early 1940. He encouraged Pete Seeger to tag along and see America as it was in the backwoods, viewed through Woody's eyes.

Almost immediately, his career skyrocketed. At a benefit for the John Steinbeck Committee for Agricultural Workers in early March, Woody met Alan Lomax, the assistant in charge of the Archive of American Folk Song at the Library of Congress. Impressed by Woody's songwriting ability, Lomax arranged for a recording session for the Library at the end of the month. Afterwards, he helped Woody secure a recording contract with Victor, which resulted in the album *Dust Bowl Ballads*. His burgeoning radio career also paralleled these recording triumphs; he even became the host of Model Tobacco's weekly program, *Pipe Smoking Time*.

This success changed Woody's life in several ways. Now, he had enough money to bring Mary and their children to New York, where they rented a comfortable apartment in uptown Manhattan. For the first time in decades, Woody was no longer living in poverty. Another change was the unaccustomed pressure of having a steady job that required him to conform to others' standards, and this restriction weighed heavily on him. Soon, he wrote, "I got disgusted with the whole sissified and nervous rules of censorship on all of my songs and ballads, and drove off down the road with Mary and the children in tow,

Woody eventually ended up in California for several months before travelling to Oregon to work for the Bonneville Power Administration as an "Information Consultant" on a documentary about the dams being built there. During this time, he wrote twenty-six songs, including "Roll On, Columbia" and "Pastures of Plenty."

In June 1941, following his month-long stint in the Pacific Northwest, Woody returned to New York City without Mary and the kids. There, he promptly joined the Almanac Singers, whose other members included Pete Seeger, Lee Hays, and Millard Lampell. They played benefits, appeared on radio programs, made albums, and sang out against "Hitlerism and fascism "and made up songs to pay honour and tribute to the story of the trade union workers around the world." Woody continued to perform with the group until late 1942, when it disbanded.

During this period, Woody's personal and professional circumstances underwent significant changes. After meeting dancer Marjorie Mazia in early 1942, the two entered a romantic relationship, and she ultimately became pregnant with his child. Unfortunately, both Woody and Marjorie were still married to other people, which led to turmoil in their lives. Woody was also working on his autobiographical novel, Bound for Glory, which, alongside his fourth child, was released around the same time in early 1943. World War II was underway when Woody first arrived in New York. After America joined the fight in late 1941, he sang songs against the Nazis, including "Round and Round Hitler's Grave" and "Reuben James." However, he became more directly engaged in the spring of 1943 when he enlisted in the Merchant Marine. He shipped out three times and was torpedoed twice.

Then, in May 1945, he was drafted into the Army just as the war was coming to a close, although he returned to civilian life by the end of the year. Earlier, while visiting home between his Merchant Marine voyages in the spring of 1944, Woody met and recorded for Moses Asch, who ran a series of independent labels that would eventually lead to the legendary Folkways Records. By 1946, Woody's family life was stronger than it had been for decades. A year earlier, he and Marjorie had finally tied the knot. While she worked as a dancer during the day, he often stayed home and played with their daughter, Cathy Ann. Unfortunately, tragedy struck in February 1947 when the little girl perished in an electrical fire. The couple soldiered on as best they could and eventually had three other children. As the 1940s drew to a close, Woody continued to participate in various benefits and wrote hundreds of songs, stories, and poems. He also made several attempts at writing another novel but struggled to concentrate for extended periods. Additionally, his behaviour, which had never aligned with society's standards, became more erratic. While his relationship with Marjorie endured until Woody stopped recording in the early 1950s, his health sadly deteriorated to the point where he faced short stints in various hospitals across New York City. Woody's condition put a terrible strain on his marriage. He was drinking to excess and behaving irrationally for some time. He and Majorie eventually parted as He was away from home so much due to hospitalisations and drifting alone.

It was in the fall of 1952, doctors at Brooklyn State Hospital diagnosed Woody as having the same condition as his mother-- Huntington's Chorea. He at first didn't want to accept the condition, and when he wasn't in the hospital, he drifted even more, visiting friends and family with little planning and often without invitation. While in the Los Angeles area in late 1952, he met a young woman named Anneke Van Kirk, and a romantic relationship blossomed, resulting in a child and marriage. However, as Woody's condition continued to deteriorate, their relationship declined, and they were soon separated.

In May 1956, Woody was committed to Greystone Park, a mental institution in New Jersey. He remained there for the next five years as his condition worsened to the point where he could no longer play the guitar, type, or even hold a pen. In the late 1950s, an admirer named Bob Gleason would pick Woody up on weekends and take him to East Orange, New Jersey, where the singer would receive visitors. It was there that Bob Dylan met Woody in early 1961. Through the efforts of Dylan and other performers such as Joan Baez and Tom Paxton throughout the 1960s, Woody's songs reached a wider audience than ever before. However, as his fame increased, so did the severity of his condition. In 1961, Marjorie moved Woody back to Brooklyn State Hospital so he could be closer to her and their children. By 1965, he could only communicate by pointing to cards reading "Yes" or "No." Finally, after almost two decades of suffering, he died on October 3, 1967.

I'm out here a thousand miles from home,
Walkin' a road other blokes have taken.
I'm seein' your world of people and things,
Your paupers, peasants, princes, and kings.

Hey, hey Woody Guthrie, I wrote you a song
'Bout a funny old world that's coming along
Seems sick and it's hungry, it's tired and it's torn
It looks like it's dying and it's hardly been born.

Hey, Woody Guthrie, but I know that you know
all the things that I'm sayin' and a-many times more
I'm a-singin' you this song, but I can't sing enough
' there's not many men that done the things that you've done.

Here's to Cisco and Sonny and Leadbelly, too
, and to all the good people who travelled with you
. Here's to the hearts and the hands of the men
that come with the dust and are gone with the wind.

I'm a-leavin' tomorrow, but I could leave today
Somewhere down the road someday
The very last thing that I'd want to do
Is to say, "I've been hittin' some hard travelin' too."

It's a thousand miles from home,
walking a road others have travelled.
I'm seeing your world of people and things,
your paupers and peasants, princes and kings.

Hey, hey Woody Guthrie, I wrote you a song
'Bout a funny ol' world that's a-comin' along
Seems sick and it's hungry, it's tired and it's torn
It looks like it's a-dyin' and it's hardly been born.

I'm a-singin' you this song, but I can't sing enough
'Cause there's not many men that done the things that you've done.

"Song to Woody", Bob Dylan.

CHAPTER 4.

LEGENDS OF FOLK SINGERS

Bob Dylan was born Robert Allen Zimmerman on May 24, 1941, and emerged as an American singer-songwriter. Regarded as one of the greatest songwriters of all time, Dylan has been a significant figure in popular culture throughout his nearly 70-year career. With an estimated 125 million records sold worldwide, he ranks among the best-selling musicians of all time. Dylan incorporated sophisticated lyrical techniques into the folk music of the early 1960s, infusing it "with the intellectualism of classic literature and poetry." His lyrics drew from political, social, and philosophical influences, defying conventions and appealing to radical music mentors like Woody Guthrie and Pete Seeger.

Bob's father, Abram Zimmerman, and his mother, Beatrice "Beatty" Stone, belonged to a small, close-knit Jewish community. They resided in Duluth until Dylan turned six, at which point his father contracted polio. Abram had been a semi-professional footballer, but after falling ill, the family moved back to his mother's hometown of Hibbing. There, they spent the rest of Dylan's childhood while his father and paternal uncles ran a furniture and appliance store.

In the early 1950s, Dylan listened to the Grand Ole Opry radio show and was introduced to the songs of Hank Williams. He later wrote: "The sound of his voice went through me like an electric rod." Dylan was also impressed by the delivery of Johnnie Ray: "He was the first singer whose voice and style, I guess, I fell in love with.. I loved his style, wanted to dress like him too."

As a teenager, Dylan heard rock and roll on radio stations broadcasting from Shreveport and Little Rock. While attending Hibbing High School, Dylan formed several bands. In the Golden Chords, he performed covers of songs by Little Richard and Elvis Presley. Their performance of Danny and the Juniors' "Rock ' n Roll Is Here to Stay" at their high school talent show was so loud that the principal cut the microphone. This was an act that Pete Seeger reportedly considered when Bob Dylan went electric at the Newport Folk Festival some years later.

On January 31, 1959, 17-year-old Dylan saw Buddy Holly perform just four days before Holly's fatal plane crash. Dylan was electrified, and in his Nobel Prize lecture, he explained: "Buddy wrote songs that had beautiful melodies and imaginative verses. And he sang great – sang in more than a few voice**s.** He was the archetype. Everything I wasn't and wanted to be." In 1959, Dylan's high school yearbook carried the caption "Robert Zimmerman: to join 'Little Richard'". That year, under the name Elston Gunn, he performed twice with Bobby Vee, playing piano and clapping. In September 1959, Dylan enrolled at the University of Minnesota. Living at the Jewish-centric fraternity Sigma Alpha Mu, Dylan began performing at the Ten O'Clock Scholar, a coffeehouse near campus, and became involved in the Dinkytown folk music scene. His focus on rock and roll shifted to American folk music, as he explained in a 1985 interview: "The thing about rock'n'roll is that for me anyway it wasn't enough.. There were great catchphrases and driving pulse rhythms, but the songs weren't serious or didn't accurately reflect life. I knew that when I got into folk music, it was more of a serious type of thing. The songs are filled with more despair, more sadness, more triumph, more faith in the supernatural, much deeper feelings."

Dylan dropped out of university in May 1960 after his first year of study. In January 1961, he travelled to New York City to perform and visit his musical idol, Woody Guthrie, at Greystone Park Psychiatric Hospital in New Jersey. Guthrie had been a revelation to Dylan and influenced his early performances. He wrote of Guthrie's impact: "The songs themselves had the infinite sweep of humanity in them... [He] was the true voice of the American spirit. I said to myself I was going to be Guthrie's greatest disciple."

In addition to Guthrie, Dylan wrote in *Chronicles* that major influences on his early songwriting included Robert Johnson's Blues and what he referred to as the "architectural forms" of Hank Williams' country songs. On August 9, 1962, Dylan legally changed his name to Robert Dylan at the St Louis County Court in Hibbing, with his father, Abraham Zimmerman, serving as the witness. Bob changed his name for several reasons; he mentioned being inspired by the poet Dylan Thomas and the jazz performer David Allyn. Initially, he had planned to go by the name Robert Allyn, but he thought that Allyn sounded too similar to Dylan, and the D carried more impact. In his memoirs, he stated that he had considered adopting the name of a street in Hibbing called Dillon until he stumbled upon poems by Dylan Thomas. This was a popular trend at the time. After all, in high school, he briefly played piano for Robert Thomas Velline's band, who later took on the stage name Bobby Vee and The Shadows. Then there was his hero, John Alvin Ray, who became Jonnie Ray, and Richard Wayne

Penniman, who became Little Richard. Given his goal to be a folk singer, it wasn't unreasonable for Bob to do this; the only surprising aspect was that his father approved the name change.

Bob Dylan met John Hammond in 1961 at a rehearsal session for folk singer Carolyn Hester. Dylan was invited to play harmonica on the session, and Hammond, impressed by his playing, decided to sign him to Columbia Records on the spot. Hammond later produced Dylan's self-titled debut album, Bob Dylan. It initially had poor sales, but Dylan became known around Columbia Studios as "Hammond's Folly." It was Hammond whose recordings, including "Blowin' in the Wind" and "A Hard Rain's a-Gonna Fall". So Hammond had the last laugh.

Dylan was introduced to Albert Grossman by Pete Seeger and signed a management contract with him, which he remained under until 1970. Grossman was known for his sometimes confrontational personality and protective loyalty. Dylan said, "He was kind of like a Colonel Tom Parker figure. You could smell him coming." Tension between Grossman and John Hammond led to the latter suggesting that Dylan work with jazz producer Tom Wilson, who produced several tracks for the second album without receiving formal credit. Wilson made the following three albums that Dylan recorded.

Before managing Bob Dylan, Albert Grossman was renowned for signing and managing other influential folk artists like Odetta, Joan Baez, and Peter, Paul and Mary. He also managed notable musicians including John Lee Hooker, Phil Ochs, Gordon Lightfoot, and Richie Havens. Many in the recording industry believed his support of Dylan was a critical mistake. Albert saw something in Bob Dylan that others could not, and in time, he was proven right. Interestingly, the now-retired Bob Dylan recently sold the rights to his songs to Sony Music for $ 400 million.

The claim that Bob Dylan stole Woody Guthrie's recordings is inaccurate. While Guthrie's music and life greatly inspired Dylan, he did not take his recordings. Dylan obtained a collection of Guthrie's records from a "red-haired spiritualist," which he used to familiarise himself with Guthrie's work. He then wrote "Song to Woody" as a tribute to Guthrie. It's clear that Dylan's early songs, recorded as covers, were heavily influenced by Woody's vocal style and melodies. Once Dylan had mastered Woody's style of play and lyrics, he returned the album collections to the bloke from whom he had borrowed them.

While Pete Seeger's influence on the Weavers' music was evident, primarily through his banjo rhythms, the group often faced criticism for being too smooth in their adaptation of older folk songs. Naturally, some people in the committees and folk music community during the 1950s and 1960s criticised others' pursuits in folk music. However, Pete Seeger was not one of those. At one particular Weavers committee meeting behind the scenes, one person was condemned for being too diverse. It was then that Woody Guthrie stood up and said: "Doesn't everyone need a little diversion now and then? "

Pete Seeger was well aware of diversity, having witnessed it firsthand within the communist left, despite the prevailing notions in the civil rights movement. Pete had gone south with Bob Dylan to participate in the civil rights movement and developed a deep respect for his artistry and poetry. He was amazed at how quickly

Dylan could write a folk song that seemed to take off without a hitch, earning public applause for his work. By the time the 1965 Newport Folk Festival rolled around, Dylan had already gone electric. Many members of the festival committee were opposed to Dylan performing. Johnny Cash had been featured in folk festivals like the Newport Folk Festival, thanks to his ability to bridge the gap between country and folk music, as well as his growing influence and crossover appeal. He explored themes related to Native American traditions in his music, which resonated with the folk audience. However, away from his acoustic guitar, Dylan and his new electric band were deemed far too loud and disconnected from folk music. Pete thought otherwise and secured the backing of enough committee members to vote in favour of his inclusion. Most had agreed because Dylan played acoustic folk and not electric.

On July 25, 1965, Pete took his father, Charles, a musicologist, to hear this incredible young man at the Newport Folk Festival. Dylan had already indicated he would perform his traditional folk using an acoustic guitar. By then, Charles was hard of hearing, a trait Pete would later inherit. Initially, Dylan played solemn early folk songs from his first album, accompanied by an acoustic guitar. It wasn't long before a group of electric musicians joined him, and even those without hearing issues found the electric guitars far too loud, drowning out the lyrics. Pete was keen for his father to hear "Maggie's Farm," but his father, struggling to make out Dylan's masterful lyrics over the loud, distorted amplification of the guitars, couldn't hear a thing. So, Pete approached the sound technician and mentioned that the guitars were too noisy.

That might not have bothered the younger audience members, but middle-aged Pete, a traditional folk music enthusiast, was incensed. The sound tech retorted, "They want it that way." Seeger was reported to have replied, "If I had an axe handy, I would cut the wires." Pete then walked away. He never got too ruffled over most things. Dylan had once called Pete, "That man is a saint." Seeger, too, like most folk musicians, was stuck in the past, while Bob seemed to move from one cause to the next and from one style of music and lyric to another. It was as if he went with the wind of change and was often ahead of the pack in this regard.

Some music historians argue that this moment marks the end of the folk boom and the start of the rock era, but nothing of the sort occurred. Rock 'n' roll had already begun before the Newport Folk Festival. Dylan had branched off from folk music, and folk music continued to thrive well after that, with Pete maintaining a lifelong respect for him.

"We all go to different churches or no churches, we have different favourite foods, different ways of making love, different ways of doing all sorts of things, but there we're all singing together. Gives you hope," said Pete Seeger.

Bob Dylan combined his knowledge of 1950s bands and blues to write in his way, and, similar to Pete Seeger, many of his songs were adopted by the civil rights movement. Armed with his youth, a characteristic not afforded to Pete Seeger during the time, Bob Dylan also helped transform American society during the 1960s. Dylan came to be because things needed saying, and he "had an ear on his generation." As the civil rights movement, the student movement, and the women's movement heated up, Bob Dylan provided a voice for what some scholars have labelled the "Age of Protest".

Through their music, both Pete Seeger and Bob Dylan created a way for people in the 1960s to unite for change in America. It wasn't just the renowned folk singing of Seeger and Dylan who urged the use of protest songs against the Vietnam War. In the early 1960s, before the anti-war movement gained significant popularity, folk singers such as Peter, Paul, and Mary (Peter Yarrow, Paul Stookey, and Mary Travers), Joan Baez, Judy Collins, Phil Ochs, and Tom Paxton conveyed the anti-war message through their music. Joan Baez was one of the first vocal opponents to criticise the Vietnam War through music, using her performances to advocate for peace during the 1960s. While Bob Dylan was also a significant figure, Baez's early contributions made her a key part of the antiwar movement.

While Bob Dylan produced several landmark protest songs, such as "Blowin' in the Wind" (1962), "Masters of War" (1963), "Talking World War III Blues" (1963), and "The Times They Are A-Changin'" (1964), in 1965, the number one hits included the frequently covered "Eve of Destruction" by Barry McGuire, which addresses the Vietnam War, politics, and the nuclear threat. The other number one hit for that year was "Draft Dodger Rag" by self-described 'singing journalist' Phil Ochs—a satirical song about draft evasion during the Vietnam War.

Phil Ochs' most notable hits, "I ain't matching any more," "There but for Fortune," and "When I'm gone," were often sung by Phil at protest concerts. His songs like "Changes," "Love Me Cause I," "Chords of Fame," and "I'm a Liberal," along with tracks from his

"Greatest Hits" album, which included "Chords of Fame" and "No More Songs," were significant. While he did not achieve the widespread chart success of Pete Seeger or Dylan, Ochs' protest songs became important cultural icons during the 1960s.

With melancholy, humour, and insight, Phil Ochs was a significant link in the chain of American songwriting. As Dave Van Ronk said: "As a lyricist, there was nobody like Phil Ochs before; there has been none since. He had a touch that was so distinctive that it could not have been anybody else. He had been a journalism student before becoming a singer, and he would never sacrifice what he felt to be true for a good line." …
In a note to Phil Ochs in 1963, Peter Seeger wrote: "I wish I had one tenth of your talent as a songwriter." Bob Dylan, commenting in a Broadside magazine in 1964, said: "I just can't keep up with Phil. And he's getting better, and better and better."

Phil had been a strong, upfront supporter of JFK, Martin Luther King, and Bobby Kennedy, and I reckon he lost his way to a great degree after their assassinations. Unfortunately, after years of prolific songwriting in the 1960s, Ochs' mental stability declined during the 1970s. He struggled with several mental health issues, including depression, bipolar disorder, and alcoholism, and he tragically died by suicide on April 9, 1976.

In my downward spiral, having lost a son to his hand, I turned to writing songs in my later years. The music for the lyrics of the following song is yet to be recorded.

A Dylan tribute dream.

Yep! Heard an old whistle sounding,
In the midnight of my mind,
saw Bob Dylan riding a boxcar,
reliving Woody Guthrie's dream.

He was singing songs of sadness,
Remembering old friends,
of the good times and the hard ones,
When Woody rode freight trains.

It was Dylan's train to glory,
on his everlasting gig,
holding on to his mortality,
Remembering how he lived.

Well, I saw the pale moon rising,
saw the light upon his face,
And his dream was in my dream,
It was for the human race.

"Oh! I saw his shooting star tonight,
watched it fade away and die,
It was in the middle of my dream,
Bob Dylan's voice just died."

Oh! The train stopped at the station,
In the crossroads of my mind,
It was then Bob Dylan alighted,
and turned his head to mine.

He was dressed in black leather,
wore Spanish leather boots,
He looked so pale and thin,
His blue eyes burned with sad tunes!

He greeted me with a grin,
And he just walked right in,
He put his guitar down by the door,
And I split a beer with him.

Dylan took over my place,
So I just hung about,
 watched him prepare a poster,
 for the epitaph of his sound.

It was a promo of his life,
with music and guitar,
In a coat of many colours,
The lyrical folk star.

And many from the other side,
began to gather round,
The man in black came in first,
And Dylan just shook his hand.

Oh! the grand ole Opry singers,
all gathered in my room,
Hank Williams strummed with Jimmy Reeves,
Chad Atkins sang an old tune.

And over in a corner,
Woody Guthrie stood alone,
strumming quietly on his guitar,
singing of some old Kentucky home!

Charlie Daniels and Tammy Wynette,
Charlie Pride and Patsy Cline,
Phil Everly and Tom T Hall,
Waiting to pick Bob Dylan's mind.

Standing by a protest poster
beside a graffiti-covered wall,
Phil Ochs stood there singing,
a song about James Dean.

"Oh! I saw his shooting star tonight,
watched it fade away and die,
It was in the middle of my dream,
Bob Dylan's voice just died."

Oh! The Kennedys were looking,
at a poster of Che Guevara,
Martin Luther King just shook his head,
Medgar Evers admired the red star!

Pete Seeger strummed an old banjo,
singing his Kum-ba-ya,
Paddy and Tom Clancy joined in,
Tommy Makem singing from afar!

Oh! There were so many faces,
to many it's plain to tell,
all gathered just for Dylan,
to give tribute and farewell.

When I awoke this morning,
I copied down this dream,
read the news today, oh! boy,
Bob Dylan's still alive.

CHAPTER 5.

PERSONAL FAVOURITES

I've been reflecting again on the musical influences in my life during the 1970s. While Pete Seeger, Bob Dylan, and Phil Ochs had a greater impact on my youth in that decade, it was the Righteous Brothers' rendition from the late 1960s that impressed me the most. I couldn't tell you why at the time, but in light of the many tragedies I endured during my childhood, this song resonates deeply with the love between two people. It symbolised the loss of a brother in arms when I was four and then again at age twelve, when my best mate drowned while we were swimming at the beach together. The lyrics of the song express the longing for a loved one. In the song, death physically separates them, yet love endures.

The influences of the Righteous Brothers' version of "Unchained Melody" and the Highwaymen's rendition of the old battle hymn, "Michael rode the boat ashore," inspired Danny and me to perform our covers of these songs around the pub scene in the early 1970s. We enjoyed a brief period of popular success, but many others doing covers also shared that experience back then. That was when I had a voice, but age and a lack of music practice have taken their toll over the years. Now, in my dotage, I return to writing and recording songs more as a hobby than anything else. [Check out YouTube Top songs Doug McPhillips if you're interested.]

Bob Dylan experienced a significant shift in his spiritual life in the late 1970s, embracing evangelical Christianity. During this period, he undertook courses at Vineyard Christian Fellowship, focusing on end-times biblical narratives and producing several gospel-influenced albums. However, his spiritual journey continued to evolve, and he later connected with Chabad, an ultra-Orthodox Hasidic Jewish movement. By his admission, he believed his musical ability and songs weren't at the level of Phil Ochs' protest songs, which Ochs wrote and recorded during his brief career.

Phil Ochs adored Bob Dylan, and Bob, back in the 1970s, was largely indifferent to other artists, except perhaps Joan Baez, with whom he sang in live performances, had a brief romance, and travelled the country like his idol Woody Guthrie, singing to audiences large and small. Bob was not one to dwell on the past. Unlike Phil Ochs, whose protest songs resonated with the public in the 1970s because they were anti-war and spoke to civil rights and the need for change, Bob Dylan frequently changed his style and continued to do so throughout his musical career. Bob wasn't one for repeating his successful songs; he continually moved on to the next trend. Phil was more like a roving singing journalist, and spent much of his time singing and campaigning for the Kennedys, as well as Martin Luther King. The assassination of these men devastated Phil, and he lost his way to a great degree after that.

In Chile, one of the most notable victims among the thousands murdered in the initial days following the 1971 coup was the popular folk singer Victor Jara, sometimes referred to as the Pete Seeger or Bob Dylan of Chile during the 60s protest phase. Yet, for three years afterwards, he remained largely unknown in the U.S., and the details of his death were debated or denied.

At *Crawdaddy* in 1974, the first significant article about Victor Jara was published in the United States. It was only because the political editor, Stew Albert (a co-founder of the Yippies), had travelled to Chile with folksinger Phil Ochs and Jerry Rubin during the waning months of Allende's rule that information about the brutal murder of Jara came to light, prompting the US public to take notice. The trio spent considerable time with Jara, and Ochs sang with him.

In an article in Crawdaddy Stew, Albert wrote that before Victor died, both Victor and Phil sang to a group of miners. Victor's songs were stirring, but he could also be playful, as seen in his rendition of a Spanish version of "Little Boxes." He had an incredible range of style and subject, and the miners would sometimes cheer and at other moments laugh. Moreover, he changed the words. Victor's "Little Boxes" was about a right-wing assassination of a loyal Allende general—it was folk music in its most valid form, created by local experience and need. Phil Ochs offered his "I Ain't Marching Anymore" declaration of independence. He sang slowly, and Victor would translate into Spanish. I don't reckon Phil ever sang to a more appreciative and supportive audience.

After the performance, Victor introduced Jerry and Stew to the audience. At first, everyone laughed or even hissed at our hair, but Victor came to our defence: "These brothers have come a long way to be with us and to support our revolution. Are we going to make them think we are cold-hearted like the rich?" Someone shouted "Viva los hippies buenos!" and everyone joined in. Afterwards, they took the elevator down into the mine. It was 2 a.m., and a group of miners who had just finished their shift came surging out. Victor was stunned by the pain on their faces. He was in a controlled rage, and his eyes filled with tears: "Look how human beings have been treated. They are made to have the expressions of animals. I tell you, man, we are going to make things different from now on."

Jara, known as the 'Bob Dylan' of Chile, was tortured and killed four days after the political assassination of the democratically elected President of Chile, Salvador Allende, on September 11, 1973, whom Jara supported. Allende, the first Democratic Socialist elected President in Chile's history, was murdered by the storm troopers of General Augusto Pinochet, with the full backing and support of US President Richard Nixon, Secretary of State Henry Kissinger, and the CIA.

Victor Jara had been, according to Clyde Haberman of the *New York Times,* "In The Life of Phil Ochs: There But for Fortune," author Michael Schumacher writes: "To Phil, Allende was the most compelling political story since the Castro-led revolution in Cuba — not to mention the kind of peaceful revolution he had dreamed about for the United States." By the summer of 1971, at the beginning of Allende's term in office, Ochs was convinced he had to go to Chile. Nothing would impact him as much as his meeting with Victor Jara in the streets of Santiago: "Although none of the Americans on the trip had heard of him before, Victor Jara was one of the most beloved populist figures in Chile — a folk singer and political activist not unlike Pete Seeger in the US. Jara had been instrumental in Allende's rise to power. His main political activity consisted of travelling around the country, singing and drumming up support for the Union Popular, which made him a folk hero among his country." A popular Chilean folk singer who dwelt on themes like poverty and injustice. He was, in no particular order, a poet, a teacher, a theatre director, a Communist Party activist, and a long-time supporter of Allende, which is what ultimately led to Jara being tortured and murdered.

It led Phil Ochs to organise an evening for the Jara family and other Chilean refugees in 1973 at the Felt Forum in Madison Square Garden, which included Arlo Guthrie and Pete Seeger, who sang; Dennis Hopper spoke; and Dylan, who boosted ticket sales, arrived late and performed three songs, one with Phil Ochs, who was famously drunk, as it happens. Victor Jara received several mentions during the evening. Later, both The Clash and U2 name-dropped him in songs.

Ironically, while Jara was frequently compared to Bob Dylan, it was Phil Ochs who, while far less famous, was much more like Jara in the United States as a political activist. Phil Ochs began his rise to modest fame around the same time Bob Dylan did, but was much more deeply enmeshed in the political activism of the early '60s than Dylan was. In 1963, Ochs travelled to Hazard, Kentucky, to perform for the families of striking coal miners; he made a pilgrimage to Mississippi in 1964 as part of the Caravan of Music to support the Freedom Fighters throughout the South. He preferred to refer to himself as a "topical songwriter and political activist," or a "musical journalist" rather than a protest singer.

While Ochs was travelling and singing for Civil Rights that summer of 1964 in Mississippi, three young civil rights workers —

Andrew Goodman, Michael Schwerner and James Chaney- were ambushed and murdered by the KKK for working to register Black citizens to vote. Ochs, distraught over the murders, wrote one of his most controversial songs: *"Here's to the State of Mississippi,"* which, along with Ochs, was banned in many Southern States. Ochs performed with Victor Jara across Chile for weeks, including at a Chilean coal mine where the working conditions were far worse than those at the Kentucky coal mines Ochs had visited eight years earlier. Once again, he performed *"Here's to the State of Mississippi"* and won over Chilean coal miners, who were sceptical of a long-haired gringo in 1970 America. [At that time, I was deeply entrenched in the workforce, leaning left in my political views, but I couldn't bring myself to protest, as a Commonwealth government department employed me. The nationwide student anti-war strike of 1970 resulted in a massive outpouring of anti-Vietnam War protests that erupted in May 1970 in response to the war's expansion into neighbouring Cambodia.

When the Pinochet goons murdered Allende and Jara in September 1973, Phil Ochs' life was already deteriorating due to worsening mental illness, alcoholism, and drug abuse. Yet, despite his struggles, Ochs *still* understood the significance of what transpired in Chile, where Fascist forces with active assistance from the United States had toppled a democratically elected government. Ochs felt isolated, forging a visceral connection with Victor Jara and the people of Chile, who just two years before his suicide at the age of 36, organised a massive *"Concert for Chile"* at Madison Square Garden in 1974 to raise money for the families of the victims of the US/Pinochet Putsch in Chile.

Ochs worked relentlessly over many months organising the *Concert for Chile*. After meeting with Bob Dylan for five hours in Ochs' own lower Manhattan apartment, he persuaded Dylan to agree to appear at the concert with Pete Seeger and Arlo Guthrie, guaranteeing a sold-out Felt Forum.

I was aware of our government's endorsement of exporting our second-grade wheat crop from Western Australia to North Vietnam, in line with the prevailing need for exports at that time. The approval of the policy to send the wheat was a contract that had to be fulfilled, as the drought in New South Wales meant we owed North Vietnam the crop to meet our international obligations. Meanwhile, our troops were still being sent to Vietnam to fight the North, and on the day my best mate John left, I couldn't help but think about the full bellies of the Vietnamese troops fighting our soldiers on the border of North and South Vietnam. The machinery used by Australian forces in Vietnam included equipment sourced from the United States, such as M113 armoured personnel carriers and helicopters like the Iroquois.

A few years later, I developed an interest in politics. As a self-employed businessman, I remained loyal to the Labour Party in state politics for quite some time before being drawn to the National Party in New England. Eventually, I became a Liberal when asked to assist in establishing a new branch of the party in the early 1980s. By that point, I was too busy providing for my family of four to concern myself with the whims of my misspent youth.

My thinking has shifted significantly over the past few years, and I have leaned more towards right-wing economic views. The plight of Aboriginal people has always left a sour taste in my mouth, yet I have remained loyal to their causes. Growing up in Country New South Wales, playing sport with Aboriginal boys and reading books like Xavier Herbert's "Capricornia," which explored the struggles of white Australians, Asians, and Aboriginals while forming profound connections amidst dispossession, betrayal, and murder, has undoubtedly influenced me deeply. Additionally, books like "The Chant of Jimmy Blacksmith" by Kennelly and the more recent cries from those of Aboriginal descent have resonated with me once more. One's bloodlines run deep, and while I take pride in my primarily Irish heritage, I cannot overlook that I have a great-grandmother who was a full-blooded Canadian Indian. Like all races, the Aboriginal connection to the land may not be what it once was, as there aren't many full-blooded Aboriginal people still living. Nevertheless, we must not forget the atrocities committed by the early British settlers, who took over the land and treated the native people like wild animals, killing many and punishing others cruelly. We cannot escape our responsibility in that regard.

Archie Roach, who passed away at the age of 66, was an Indigenous Australian singer-songwriter, guitarist, and writer. His most famous song, "Took the Children Away," describes his own painful life story and, in the process, helps educate Australians about one of the darkest chapters in history. Artists such as Yothu Yindi, Warumpi Band, and Archie Roach have created music that reflects the lives, struggles, and cultural heritage of Aboriginal and Torres Strait Islander peoples. John Schumann is known for his song "On Every Anzac Day," which pays tribute to Indigenous soldiers and acknowledges their contributions to war efforts. Midnight Oil also produced "The Dead Heart," which addresses the mistreatment of Aboriginal and Torres Strait Islanders and the impact of stolen land.

Kevin Carmody's "From the Land" is a folk epic about the Gurindji Strike, a ten-year civil rights campaign that led to the introduction of the Aboriginal Land Rights Act. Many First Nations artists, including Emily Wurramara, Isaiah Firebrace, Miesha, and Baker Boy, contribute to the diverse landscape of Australian music, often addressing issues relevant to their communities. Musicians like Dave Arden and Paul Kelly co-wrote "Freedom Called" to honour Aboriginal Anzacs, showcasing a collaborative effort towards reconciliation.

Still, one must admire those who have the foresight to move beyond the past. Let go of old causes; accept the freedom of being in the now. In light of my thoughts about those folk singers of the past, it's challenging to overlook the efforts of Bob Dylan and his songwriting ability to shift to new causes throughout his seventy-year musical career—something Phil Ochs failed to do. Phil Ochs seems caught up in seeking recognition due to his abandonment as a child, while Dylan had already moved on from that need and set his sights on broader fields of endeavour.

I came to learn more about Phil Ochs during my latter years and wrote a song about him for my first album, released in 2014; the lyrics of which are included here.

Phil Ochs, folk singer.

Once there was a boy
from an old El Paso town,
loved his life and family.

Father came back from the war,
a torn and shattered man
Mother turned her back
on them.

He graduated from military school,
gave up university,
took off
to New York City,

The goal was political left,
Civil rights was his cause
Phil Ochs was here and there
for peace.

He worked the streets often alone
singing protest songs he wrote,
about the latest news
and current events

In the streets of Greenwich Village.
He organised protest rallies
Phil Ochs was there
to stop a war.

Once there was a folk singer,
who busked out on the street,
He sang out with a cause,
for peace,

a voice without fame,
stood ragged in the rain,
Seemed to him his cause
was lost."

Sang for Martin Luther King,
Did the same for JFK
saw him as the Father
of the nation.

But the bullets came so fast
and in their dying gasp
The words of peace
their epithet

He renewed his faithful plea,
worked for Bobby Kennedy
The one last hope
for liberty

But the night the shot rang out
folk singer died some that day
another hero
lying in his grave

Once there was a folk singer
Who busked out on the street
He sang out with a cause
for peace

A voice without fame
stood ragged in the rain
seemed to him his cause
was lost.

Phil tuned up his guitar
When he met Victor Jara'
The heroic Chilean
folk singer

They sang of the need for change
Life was being rearranged
Life was coming to an end
for them.

 Oh! The moon turned blood red
When Salvador Chile fell,
a victim
of a coup d'état,

It was on that fateful night
Victor Jara lost his life
Chile's voice of peace
was dead

 Phil Ochs rose to the cause.
A concert to end wars,
the benefit
for the Jar'a family.

So he sang his final song
And he left this mortal coil
a sad theme
It was his last song.

CHAPTER 6.

THE RADIO STARS

Pete Seeger's banjo skills were developed through a combination of exposure and apprenticeship with Appalachian folk musicians. His initial exposure to the instrument came from a trip to the Mountain Dance and Folk Festival in Asheville, North Carolina, where he first heard the five-string banjo. He then learned directly from Bascom Lamar Lunsford, the festival organiser and a renowned banjoist, who even lent Seeger a banjo to learn on. Seeger further honed his skills by seeking out and learning from other old-time pickers he met along his travels.

Charles Seeger invited Lunsford to their home in Washington, D.C., where Pete received a brief introduction to Lunsford's "Lunsford style" of playing. He further developed his signature "basic strum" technique to accompany his singing, focusing on the lyrics and rhythm. He also pioneered the "longneck banjo" by modifying his instrument for broader chord ranges and lower notes.

Pete Seeger learned 12-string techniques from Lead Belly and credited him as his "silent music teacher." Lead Belly's influence also extended to Seeger's musical style, as he later adopted and popularised Lead Belly's unique mix of blues, folk, gospel, and country sounds. Peter later wrote a book and released an instructional LP, using Lead Belly as a model for learning and playing the 12-string guitar. Pete Seeger's book on how to play the banjo was titled "How to Play the 5-String Banjo." It was initially self-published in 1948 and has been reprinted multiple times since then. It featured a unique playing style—rather than initially hitting a string with a downward stroke from the back of a fingernail of his right hand, Pete developed what became known as the Seeger "basic strum" or "up picking."

Pete Seeger co-founded the Almanac Singers in 1940 with Lee Hays and Millard Lampell. The group later included Woody Guthrie, Sis Cunningham, Bess Lomax, and Sonny Terry. Pete's banjo skills formed the backbone of the group. He co-founded the Almanac Singers to promote progressive causes, including industrial unionisation, racial and religious inclusion, and various social issues. They sang on the radio and recorded a union song, "Which side are you on?", followed by Woody Guthrie's "This land is your land," which ultimately resonated with audiences across the country. They continued to record until after the Almanac Singers disbanded, and Seeger pursued his musical career by forming The Weavers with Lee Hays and others after the war.

When Woody joined Pete, they were involved with the American Peace Mobilisation (APM), a group backed by the Communist Party, and their songs reflected their political views. The Almanac Singers, as a folk music group that included Pete Seeger and Woody Guthrie, disbanded primarily due to the prevailing political climate and the influence of McCarthyism. The group's left-leaning views, particularly their songs and activism in support of workers' and civil rights, led to accusations of Communist affiliation and scrutiny by government committees. Pete Seeger and other members of the Weavers were called to testify before the House Un-American Activities Committee, a government body that investigated alleged communist activities. Pete had claimed that he had never been a member of the Communist Party, but refused to deny the accusations and scrutiny. Pete Seeger refused to sign a pledge condemning communism to be allowed to perform a concert. Specifically, he refused to sign an oath stating that his concert would not promote communism or an overthrow of the government. He also refused to plead the Fifth Amendment, which would have suggested that his testimony might be self-incriminating. He had taken the view that his political views were his right under the constitution and were no one else's business.

The resulting blocklisting of many performers, including the Weavers, led to challenges in finding gigs and opportunities. The pressure and negative publicity resulted in the group's disbandment in 1952. While the Almanac Singers disbanded due to members joining the military during the US involvement, and similarly The Weavers, due to the Senator McCarthy witch hunt, the group's legacy continued through the individual careers of its members, particularly Pete Seeger, who went on to have a long and influential career in folk music and activism. For a long time, the only work Pete could find as a singer-songwriter was teaching children in schools and performing at universities across Australia. He wrote extensively on how to play the banjo and taught many young people how to play.

In the meantime, he headed west with Woody to the panhandle in Texas. Along the way, he learnt how to survive with little or no money. Pete picked up from Woody how to hop on freight trains for a free ride to the next town. Woody had said, *"Pete, when you arrive in a country town, sling your banjo over your shoulder, make your way to a saloon bar and buy a nickel beer, and drink it slowly. Sooner or later, someone will come to you and say, ' Hey Kid, can you play that thing?' Don't be too eager. Say,' Well, maybe a little, but keep on sipping your beer. ' Sooner or later, someone will say,' Hey Kid, I got a quarter for you if you pick me a tune. ' Then you swing around and play your best song. With that kind of instruction, I couldn't go wrong.*

While on their way to Texas to visit Woody's wife, Peter recalled how they stopped off in Oklahoma City to attend a union-organised oil drillers' meeting. There were about sixty members in the room, including their wives and children. It was clear they were short of money and wanted better terms; they also couldn't afford babysitters while at the meeting. Then six men in overcoats walked in and stood along the back wall, and the union organiser said, "I don't know who they are or what they want, and they might be intent on breaking up this meeting, so see if you can get the crowd singing." Soon enough, Woody and I had the crowd singing along with the women and children. And sure enough, the heavies said, "Yeah, we did intend to break this up, but this is a little different than what we were told." They had clubs underneath their overcoats. Then they said, "You should have an American flag next time you have a meeting," but they never did break up the meeting. As Pete told it, after the meeting, one person approached Woody and said, *'All of your songs are about men, what about a song for women?' The very next morning in the union office, Woody was at the typewriter, tapping out verses tuned to his guitar. He had taken an old German song called 'Happy Plowman' and turned it into a song called the Union Maid. He wrote that song in a matter of minutes.* Woody and Peter hitchhiked on credit. Woody paid a down payment on a car in New York, then drove it to Texas to visit his wife. On his return to New York, he got a contract to record songs for Victor Records, and that's when he recorded the Dust Bowl Ballad.

Pete was later hitchhiking through New York State and ended up living with a mate on the East Side of New York. There he caught up with Woody, who borrowed his typewriter for one night, and that's when he wrote the song about The Grapes of Wrath. The screenplay writer had condensed the book into a three-hundred-page, one-and-a-half-hour movie. Overnight, Woody managed to condense the whole thing into a six-minute song called "Tom Joad." It was on a 78 rpm recording, so half the song was on one side of the record and the other half of the song went on the opposite side.

In the late 1940s, new formats pressed in vinyl, the 45 rpm single and 33 rpm long playing "LP", were introduced, gradually overtaking the formerly standard "78s" over the next decade. The late 1950s saw the introduction of stereophonic sound on commercial discs. My dad's era featured 78 rpm records before the transition from shellac to vinyl. Radio grams were all the rage back then, and we could listen to our LP (extended play) record collection, which could hold a whole album of six or more songs. Over time, the LP brand has been associated with CDs or digital releases. In the 1950s, songs were recorded in analog format and had greater clarity than the digital recordings of today. Back then, a record player typically had a spindle that could hold and automatically play a stack of records, allowing for continuous playback and enabling a continuous listening experience.

The radio was our primary source of music to listen to, as TV was not introduced in Australia until the end of the 1950s. As a result, the Weavers' songs became popular during that era, to which I, too, was exposed.

Reflecting on it now, Pete shared a wealth of stories about his mate Woody Guthrie during an interview about his time with the travelling singer. He reminisced about the formation of the Almanac Singers in early 1941 and Woody's role in the group. Woody Guthrie had been out west singing songs about the Grand Coulee Dam. Pete wrote him a letter inviting him to join along with Lee Hays and his flatmate, Millard Lampell, who were forming The Almanac Singers. The trio had written a song, 'The Ballad of Harry Bridge,' and Pete did the banjo work. Woody hitchhiked back east to join them. They were all left-leaning and sang for the unions at Madison Square Garden to support the striking transit workers.

Woody had deserted his wife too many times, so she returned to Texas to obtain a divorce. Meanwhile, Woody, looking for a place to stay, knocked on Pete's door. It was June 23rd; Hitler had invaded the Soviet Union the day before, and Woody's first words were: "I guess we won't be singing peace songs, will we?" Churchill had turned from wanting to strangle the Bolshevik baby in the cradle.

To support the Soviets. Woody said:" Yep. Churchill has flip-flopped, so we have to flip-flop too." So it was that Peter and Woody stuck to union songs as they criss-crossed the country.

The Almanac Singers had recorded 'The Ballad of Harry Bridges' at the request of the Harry Bridges Defence Committee, six weeks before Pete and Woody hit the road again. "HarryBridge" likely refers to prominent Australian-born American labour leader Harry Bridges, not a specific event or concept. Bridges was a key figure in the International Longshore and Warehouse Union (ILWU) and is well known for his leadership during the 1934 West Coast maritime strike. He was also a target of government scrutiny and persecution due to his association with the Communist Party and his left-wing views.

The Almanacs all piled into an old car and drove west, stopping briefly to sing for the seamen's convention in Ohio, then moved on to the Chicago Repertory Theatre for a concert. After that, they headed to Denver, Salt Lake City, and then on to Reno. They arrived in San Francisco just in time to sing at a meeting of Local 10. The 1940s were a period of significant labour organisation and union activity in the United States, including the formation of many Local unions, such as Local 10. These Local unions played a crucial role in collective bargaining, representing workers in specific industries or workplaces and advocating for better wages, working conditions, and benefits. They sang the ballad of Harry Bridges and got a standing ovation. They had to sing it twice through. The crowd were slapping Woody so hard on the back they nearly knocked him over. He was a small man, standing no more than five feet four inches. They sang it up and down the West Coast, from Los Angeles to San Francisco, Portland, Oregon, and Seattle. A few months later, Woody wrote the "Sinking of the Ruben James ", which still proves popular today with old folkies. By 1941, the Almanacs had expanded to include Bess Lomax, Butch Haws, and Sis Cunningham.

Meanwhile, Woody felt that everyone in the world was essential and the names of those men who went down on the Ruben James should be mentioned, so he got busy writing verses that included the names of the forty men who had drowned. He sang it to the Almanacs, and they all agreed that nobody but Woody was going to sing those verses. Woody grumbled and grumbled about that, but he gave the group a chorus that they could all join in on.

*"What were the names,
Tell me what the names were
Did you have a friend on the good Ruben James?"*

Woody was not just a fine musician; he was a wordsmith of the finest order. Although he usually started his songs with words first and got the tune later. He once said, *'I write some words, then look around for an old tune that people seem to like and fit the tune.'* The Almanac Singers recorded peace and union songs in 1940, and after Hitler invaded the Soviet Union and the rest of the world was drawn into the conflict, they stopped singing strike songs and sang songs to 'win the war' for the next three and a half years. The Communist Party influenced the labour movement at the time, and the Almanacs placed their emphasis on doing a good job to defeat Hitler. Pete got married in July 1943, and his wife, Toshi, joined him, living off the army base. Pete then went overseas, and Woody joined the merchant navy.

After the war ended, Seeger moved back to New York City and invited a loose-knit group of musicians to sing together in his basement. Known as the People's Songs, the group picked up where the Almanac Singers left off, working to support progressive causes, including Henry Wallace's 1948 presidential bid. Fred Hellerman and Ronnie Gilbert, the other two original members of the Weavers, were part of the People's Songs. The group came together after Wallace's defeat (Jackie Wilson, a fifth member of the group, dropped out before they began performing together). Calling themselves the No-Name Quartet, the group struggled to secure gigs and make a living during their first year. Their big break came when they were booked for two weeks in December at the Village Vanguard, a jazz club in New York's Greenwich Village.

By then, having renamed themselves the Weavers after an obscure 19th-century German play, they were a hit with audiences. Jazz club owner Max Gordon asked them back for a six-month run. They were paid $250 a week, more than they had ever earned before. They also signed a record deal with Decca Records, and in the summer of 1950, they released "Goodnight Irene," a song that gave the Weavers a national audience. The song was first recorded by Huddie "Lead Belly" Ledbetter in 1933. He sang the song to Pete Seeger (perhaps) while teaching him his style of 12-string guitar.

The group had a massive hit in 1950 with Leadbelly's "Goodnight Irene," followed by the 1941 song "Tzena, Tzena Tzena," which then became a bestseller. In keeping with audience expectations of the time, these and other early Weavers releases included violins and orchestration alongside the group's string-band instruments.

On Feb 9, 1950, Wisconsin Senator Joseph McCarthy delivered a speech at the McLure Hotel in Wheeling, West Virginia, during which he claimed to possess a list of known communists ("enemies from within") in the U.S. State Department. Due to the escalating Red Scare of the early 1950s, their manager, Pete Cameron, advised them against performing their most explicitly political songs and encouraged them to avoid progressive venues and events. Consequently, some folk song fans accused them of diluting their beliefs and commercialising their singing style. However, the Weavers believed it was worthwhile to share their songs with the public.

During the Red Scare, Pete Seeger and Lee Hays were denounced as Communist Party members by FBI informant Harvey Matusow. (who later recanted) and ended up being called up to testify to the

House Committee on Un-American Activities in 1955. Hays took the Fifth Amendment. Pete Seeger, however, refused to answer on First Amendment grounds, denying that he was ever a member of the Communist Party, the first to do so after the conviction of the Hollywood film industry's known members of the Communist Party in 1950. Seeger was found guilty of contempt and placed under restrictions by the court pending appeal. However, in 1961, his conviction was overturned on constitutional grounds, effectively ending the committee's power. Because Seeger was among those listed in the entertainment industry publication, all of the Weavers were placed under FBI surveillance and not allowed to perform on television or radio during the McCarthy era. Decca Records terminated their recording contract and deleted their songs from their catalogue in 1953; as a result, their records were denied airplay, which dried up their income from royalties.. As a result, the group's economic viability diminished rapidly, and in 1952, it disbanded. After this, Pete Seeger continued his solo career, although like all, he continued to suffer from the blocklisting.

Burl Ives was a highly popular folk singer known for songs like "Big Rock Candy Mountain" and "On Top of Old Smoky." Burl Ives gained fame in the 1940s and 1950s. He was also associated with The Almanac Singers for a time. While both Peter Seeger and Burl Ives were initially part of the same folk music circle, Ives's statement to the House Un-American Activities Committee (HUAC) led to a rift and criticism from Seeger and other folk singers. Burl Ives testified before the House Un-American Activities Committee, naming other individuals as possible communists. This act, while helping him escape blocklisting and continue his acting career, angered many in the folk music community, including Pete Seeger. Burl Ives went on to Broadway roles and Oscar-winning movie performances, not to mention stature as the face of American folk music until the emergence of Bob Dylan in the early '60s.

Forty-one years later, on May 17, 1993, the bitterness finally came to an end. The then-ailing Burl Ives, 84, and Pete Seeger, 74, were reunited for a benefit concert in New York City. They sang "Blue Tail Fly" together. After Burl Ives died in 1995, Pete Seeger praised his tenor voice and the role it played in preserving many vital American songs.

In December 1955, the Weavers reunited for a sold-out concert at Carnegie Hall. The concert was a massive success, and an independent label, Vanguard Records, released a recording of the performance, which led to their signing with that label. By the late 1950s, Mccarthyism was on the decline, and the Weavers enjoyed renewed popularity. In the late fifties, however, they agreed to provide vocals for a TV cigarette commercial. Opposed to the dangers of tobacco and disheartened by the group's apparent sell-out to commercial interests, Pete Seeger chose to resign. He spent his last year with the Weavers, honouring his commitments, but described feeling like a prisoner. He left the group on April 1, 1958.

Weavers celebrated the group's 15th anniversary with two nights of concerts at Carnegie Hall in March 1963. Folksinger" The group disbanded in 1964, but Gilbert, Hellerman and Hays occasionally reunited with either Seeger or Darling into 1980. Lee Hays, ill and using a wheelchair, wistfully approached the original Weavers for one last get-together. Hays's informal picnic prompted a professional reunion and a triumphant return to Carnegie Hall. A documentary film, "The Weavers: Wasn't That A Time!" (1982), was released after Hays's death and chronicled the history of the group, as well as the events leading up to the reunion.

Lee Hays died in 1981, and his biography, *Lonesome Traveller,* by Doris Willens, was published in 1988. In February 2006, The Weavers received the Lifetime Achievement Award given out annually at the Grammy Awards show. Represented by members Ronnie Gilbert and Fred Hellerman, they struck a chord with the crowd as they recounted their struggles with political witch hunts during the 1950s. "If you can exist, and stay the course -- not a course of blind obstinacy and faulty conception -- but one of decency and good sense, you can outlast your enemies with your honour and integrity intact," said Hellerman.

It was raining mighty hard on that Capitol yard
When the young folks gathered at the White House gate
And the President raised his hand and said to the young folks:
 Tell me, why do you stand there in the rain?

Why do you stand there in the rain?
Why do you stand there in the rain?
These are strange goings-on on the White House Capitol lawn
Tell me, why do you stand there in the rain?

Well, they tell me they've lands where they won't let you stand in the rain and ask for jobs on the lawn.
Thank God, in the USA, you can stand there every day
But I could not guarantee they'll take you in,
-
- Woody Guthrie

CHAPTER 7.

CENTRES OF INFLUENCE

Pete Seeger not only recounted his travels with Woody Guthrie, absorbing his musical talents, including his knack for picking a tune in any key, but also highlighted Woody's immense intellect. He remarked to Pete that even at six years old, Woody was reading books in the library that were well beyond his years. Adults typically read such books, and he was merely a child. The librarian would ask, "Have you read this? " Woody usually replied, 'I've already read it, ' yet he kept coming back for more books; he was a voracious reader. He told Pete about his visits to his mother in the mental institution, where she didn't recognise him. The medical profession understood little about memory loss, and Woody was devastated to see her in that condition. For the following three years, he lived with his uncle, a musician, and during that time, he likely learnt to play the guitar, the banjo, and the fiddle.

It was during Pete's collaboration with Guthrie that Woody was visiting Pete's sister-in-law in New York. Woody had noticed a book by French writer François Rabelais in English, and he borrowed it for an overnight read. A day or two later, he sensed the author's ideas, naming adjectives by the dozens. If he had come from an intellectual family, he might have pursued academics, but music was his true passion. He was convinced that he could reach people best that way. The prose we know you read once or twice, but the music you play forever. Woody was what you might call streetwise, and he taught Pete a lot in this regard.

The Weavers marked a pivotal moment in Pete Seeger's life, as it was his first taste of commercial success and introduced folk music to a national radio audience. While he avoided the excesses of fame, his desire to communicate his ideals was expressed through his music. By November 1948, the Weavers' unique blend of singing and international folk dancers at a fundraiser for the People's Song Bulletin had them practising weekly for their next gig on the radio. At that time, Pete was out of work and approached Max Gordon of The Village Vanguard to perform for $200 a week and free hamburgers. Max extended the Weavers' initial two-week engagement. The crowds grew each week, leading to the renewal of their engagement time and again, which is how the group met Gordon Jenkins, a band leader at Decca, who signed their first record deal. They achieved success, particularly with the release of "Irene, Goodnight," which became a worldwide hit.

At that time, Pete was earning a steady income from the rise in popularity of The Weaver's songs. So, he borrowed enough money to purchase seventeen acres of land on a hillside overlooking the Hudson River at Beacon. He effectively built his own home with the help of his newlywed wife, Toshi, and some mates. He reportedly used a plan he found in a library book, cut down trees, built a log cabin with assistance from a German stone mason, and enlisted friends to lift logs and move them into place. It was 1949, and for a time, things were looking bright.

So, a little trip down memory lane is essential to gather the missions of these folk singers, the Weavers, and those who were influential in their success. As John Donne's famous poem says, "No man is an island unto himself; he is a part of the whole," and it would be remiss of me not to mention those others who influenced Pete Seeger in his early years as a folk singer apart from family. Mentors in Pete's life fill in the blanks that could easily be overlooked while telling this tale. We know that Leadbelly played a role in encouraging Pete and teaching him songs. If it weren't for Leadbelly's "Irene Goodnight," which became a hit song for the Weavers in 1948, they may have faded away just like their predecessor group, the Almanac Singers. The career of Pete's father paralleled that of John Lomax, an American teacher who pioneered musicology and folklore in the latter decades of the 19th century and through the first four decades of the 20th century. John and his son, Alan, made significant contributions to preserving American folk music and served as stewards of the folk archives until 1933. Alan Lomax was an American ethnomusicologist best known for his extensive field recordings of folk music during the 20th century. He was a musician, folklorist, archivist, writer, scholar, political activist, oral historian, and filmmaker. Peter Seeger was just nineteen when he worked with Alan Lomax at the Library of Congress, assisting in the Archive of American Folk Song, and they collaborated on collecting and preserving folk music. Lomax also played a key role in introducing Seeger to Woody Guthrie and the Almanac Singers. Both Lomax and Seeger were passionate about using music to connect with people and promote social change, making them natural collaborators. Alan Lomax's legacy in the Alan Lomax Library includes 5,000 hours of sound recordings, 400,000 feet of motion picture film, 2,450 videotapes, 2,000 scholarly books and journals, hundreds of photographic prints and negatives, and over 120 linear feet of manuscripts.

Walt Whitman's celebration of the working-class hero. In *Leaves of Grass,* Whitman dreams of a race of singers who will celebrate the working class as the heart of American democracy. It was Alan Lomax who inspired Woody Guthrie, Pete Seeger, Bob Dylan, and many other folk singers to bring the mission that Whitman spoke of to life during those years, marked by songs against war, the Civil Rights movement, peace marches, and environmental preservation. It was Alan Lomax who enlisted the talents of the likes of Pete Seeger and fellow musicians **to** bring messages of radical change to the public eye in a style that set the world thinking. Lomax once said, *"There is an impulsive and romantic streak in my nature that I find difficult to control when I go song hunting."* His love for poets like Carl Sandburg influenced the prose style of his writings on music and dance. Scorning what he called "chair-bound scholars," he pursued an unending journey in search of truth and beauty that he found in folksong and dance.

Pete formed the folk group The Weavers with Ronnie Gilbert, Lee Hays, and Fred Hellerman in 1948, before he built the log cabin. The Weavers were the most influential and popular folk music group in the United States from 1949 to 1951, selling millions of records and attracting a large following. Here's a brief overview of each of the other original members of The Weavers, providing the reader with further insight into the backgrounds and personalities that attracted Pete to collaborate with them as a musician at the time.

Ruth Alice "Ronnie" Gilbert (September 7, 1926 - June 6, 2015) was born into a Jewish family. Ronnie's mother was Polish, and her father came from Ukraine, where Jews were prohibited from owning land. She grew up in New York and possessed a strong sense of justice. She was nearly expelled from high school due to her refusal to participate in a blackface minstrel show with white students, citing Paul Robeson's "denunciations of racism." Gilbert moved to Washington, D.C., during World War II at the age of 16, took a government job, and joined a protest folk-singing group called the Priority Ramblers. She performed with this group before founding the Weavers alongside Pete Seeger. After returning to New York, Gilbert became involved in organising the Office Workers' Union and worked for the Textile Workers' Union. She encountered Library of Congress folklorist Alan Lomax, Woody Guthrie, and other folk singers. She had a bold, crystalline contralto voice that blended well with male vocals but could reach a high pitch when necessary to sing above the men. Following the Weavers' dissolution in 1953 due to the blocklist, she continued her activism on a personal level, travelling to Cuba in 1961 on a trip that brought her back to the United States on the same day that country banned travel to Cuba. She also participated in the 1968 Parisian protest after travelling to that country to work with British theatrical director Peter Brook.

In 1968, Gilbert appeared on Broadway for a time in a dramatic musical, then later moved to Berkeley. In 1971, she entered graduate school and began her career as a psychologist in 1974. In 1980, the Weavers reunited for a film, and in 1984, she joined Pete Seeger and Arlo Guthrie for the album HARP (an acronym for "Holly, Arlo, Ronnie, and Pete"). In 1986, Gilbert wrote and appeared in a one-woman show about Mary Harris "Mother" Jones, the Irish-American activist and labour organiser, and a second work based on author Studs Terkel's book, *Coming of Age.* In her portrayal of Jones, Gilbert aimed to portray a woman who was at once "spunky and sarcastic, fearless and opinionated". The show's songs, most of which were written by Gilbert, provide insight into a time of resistance to injustice in the United States. Like the other members of the group, Ronnie had left-wing political sympathies and suffered when the group was blocked in the FBI's anti-communist campaigns of the 1950s. But the music endured, and Gilbert continued with the group through several personnel changes and reunions.

Lee Hays (1914-1981) was best known as the bass singer in the Weavers. Historian Studs Terkel noted that the Weavers were responsible for "entering folk music into the mainstream of American life." Among the songs he is most known for are: "If I Had a Hammer," "Roll the Union On," "Raggedy, Raggedy, Are We," "The Rankin Tree," "On Top of Old Smoky," "Kisses Sweeter than Wine," and "Goodnight Irene." Lee Hays was born on March 14, 1914, to a strict Methodist preacher, William Benjamin Hays, and Ellen Reinhardt Hays. At that time, Hays's father was serving as the editor of the *Arkansas Methodist,* but later returned to the pulpit. By the time Hays turned twelve, he had lived in five different towns across Arkansas and completed high school in Georgia while his father travelled the Methodist circuit.

Hays spent much of his life rebelling against his father's fundamentalism; he took up smoking and drinking at a young age and never stopped. However, his church background added a profound religious element to his singing and songwriting. Some claimed Hays's political principles had a fundamentalist quality of their own. Hays became a student at Commonwealth College in the late 1930s, during the Great Depression in the United States. The rural college located near Mena was committed to assisting working men by promoting the organisation of labour unions. Hays was appalled by the hardships suffered by southern sharecroppers and labourers and believed that union activism was essential to American workers.

At Commonwealth, Hays dressed in overalls, attended labour-oriented classes, and worked with fellow students in the fields. New York playwright Eli Jaffe, a student alongside him, recalled that Hays was "deeply religious and extremely creative and imaginative and firmly believed in the Brotherhood of Man." Hays also preached in local churches and wrote songs, plays, and stories. He transformed hymns and negro spirituals into songs about unions, sometimes substituting the word "union" for "Jesus." His labour-related ballads delighted his contemporaries so much that they raised sixty-five dollars to send him to New York City for a larger audience. In New York, Hays met Pete Seeger, another young political singer who became his lifelong friend and collaborator. Together, they dreamed of using folk music—the traditional music of low-income people—to achieve their political goals. Lee Hays significantly contributed to folk music by bringing songs of the labour movement and social justice to a broader audience, particularly through his work with The Weavers. He also played a key role in popularising traditional folk songs and spirituals, sometimes adapting them to address social and political issues. Lee Hays died on August 26, 1981, from diabetic cardiovascular disease at his home in Croton, New York. He had previously undergone amputations of both legs due to complications from diabetes.

Fred Hellerman (13 May 1927—1 September 2016) was a guitarist, producer, and songwriter with The Weavers. He was born on May 13, 1927, in Brooklyn, New York to Jewish parents and was the youngest of three children. His father, Harry, was an immigrant from Latvia, and his mother, Clara, was born in the United States to parents who were also immigrants from Riga. In

1949, he earned a Bachelor of Arts degree from Brooklyn College and co-wrote hits with Lee Hays. He used a pseudonym to protect his identity due to his involvement with left-wing groups in the 1930s and 1940s. Like Pete Seeger and Lee Hays, Hellerman came under suspicion of having communist sympathies during the McCarthy era. In 1950, he and the rest of the Weavers were named in the anti-communist tract "Red Channels" and placed on the industry blocklist. In February 1952, an FBI informant testified that the Weavers were members of the Communist Party.

The group, unable to perform on television, radio, or in most music halls, disbanded in 1952 but resumed singing in 1955. They continued performing together until 1963, despite personnel changes. Fred also played on Joan Baez's eponymous first album in 1960. The Weavers held several reunion concerts in 1980, just before Hays' death. Fred Hellerman, under the pseudonym Fred Brooks, adapted "Green Grow the Lilacs" for Harry Belafonte's 1959 album, Love Is a Gentle Thing. The song, rooted in a traditional Irish tune popular in the 19th-century United States, received new lyrics, including two original verses penned by Hellerman, who also reworked the chorus. He married the writer Susan Lardner in 1970. The Hellermans had two children, Caleb and Simeon, and three grandchildren. Fred Hellerman was the last surviving original member of the Weavers. He passed away on 1 September 2016, at his home in Weston, Connecticut, at the age of 89.

Unfortunately, the Weavers' success coincided with the McCarthy era. They were blocked and placed under surveillance due to the political beliefs of some of their members. As a result, they were barred from television, gigs were cancelled, and radio stations refused to play their music. They disbanded in 1952 but reunited in

1955 after a staged Carnegie Hall reunion of the band sold out. Among the audience on December 24, 1955, were individuals who later formed the Limeliters, the Kingston Trio, Peter, Paul and Mary, and Mitch Miller. Mary Travers of Peter, Paul and Mary later credited the Weavers for the success and the very existence of her folk group. Among the albums the Weavers released were *"Wasn't That a Time"*, *"Union Songs"*, *"Talking Union"*, *"Sod Buster Ballads"*, *"Deep Sea Chanteys"*, *"Gospel"*, *"Best of the Weavers"*, *"Goodnight Irene"*, *"Kisses Sweeter Than Wine"*, and *"Together Again."*

After being blocked and convicted of contempt of Congress, Peter struggled to find regular work as a folk singer. He had worked tirelessly to teach children in schools across America how to play the banjo and sing songs, always with the audience leading, always accompanied by his vocals, banjo playing, and guitar. He was an authentic Pied Piper in that regard.

Pete was a co-founder of the Newport Folk Festival in 1960, and the lineup emphasised music diversity, booking performers from Africa, Scotland, Spain, Israel, and Ireland alongside "traditional" folk musicians such as Seeger himself, Ewan MacColl, and John Le Hooper. Cisco Houston and Tommy Makem. The Newport Folk Festival has a rich connection to protest movements. In the '60s, the festival became a platform for artists who played a substantial part in the civil rights and anti-war movements, including Pete Seeger, Arlo Guthrie, Joan Baez, Tom Paxton, Sweet Honey in the Rock, and the Staple Singers. The festival, held from July 26 to 28, 1963, was a landmark event in the history of folk music. Peter was the elder statesman who performed. The festival included Bob

Dylan and Peter, Paul and Mary. Paul and Mary, Joan Baez, and Pete had been tireless in their efforts to make it a success.

In 1962, two young members of the Student Nonviolent Coordinating Committee formed a gospel vocal quartet known as The Freedom Singers. Pete and Toshi Seeger assisted the Freedom Singers in organising a nationwide college tour. As a result, the civil rights movement was deeply embraced by the folk music community. In 1963, the Freedom Singers performed on the first night of the Newport Folk Festival, and on the second night, Joan Baez joined SNCC activists and around 600 festival-goers on a march through Newport. The crowd walked past the Bellevue Avenue mansions and into Touro Park, where SNCC's executive secretary, James Forman, and Freedom Singers leader Cordell Reagan delivered speeches, rallying support for the March on Washington scheduled for the following year.

For the final performance on Friday, let Bob Dylan close the night with a set of particularly topical songs: "With God on Our Side", "Talkin' John Birch Society Blues", and "A Hard Rain's Gonna Fall". Peter, Paul, and Mary then returned to perform an encore of "Blowin' in the Wind." Amidst a "deafening roar of applause," they brought to the stage in support of Dylan, Joan Baez, Pete Seeger, Theo Bikel, and the Freedom Singers. The singers formed a single line, facing the audience with their arms crossed and hands clasped, and began to sing a variation of the Baptist hymn "I'll Overcome Someday." The hymn's new incarnation—"We Shall Overcome"—had become an anthem for the Civil Rights Movement.

In 1963, Peter Seeger embarked on a 10-month world tour with his family in tow, which included a visit to Australia. In September of that year, his performances were well-received, with sold-out shows and positive feedback from the audience. Seeger returned to Australia in 1968, continuing to inspire the folk music community and participating in significant events, such as the Sydney Town Hall concert. He also toured extensively through the British Isles, returning with songs from his travels and performing in various venues. Seeger's 1963 tour was pivotal in sparking the folk music revival in Australia, with his music and songbooks gaining popularity among aspiring musicians. His performances were noted for creating a strong sense of community and collective singing, fostering a sense of "we" among the audience. Throughout the 1960s, Seeger's music played a significant role in the Civil Rights Movement.

Peter, Paul and Mary's Paul Stookey said of Pete Seeger, "He lived simply, with modesty, and suffered most compliments warily. I never had a conversation with him that did not include some expression of hope, some praise for a stand well taken, whether political or environmental, and always underpinned by his longstanding belief in the equity of humankind. Pete was all about community, and singing together was the 'golden thread' with which he wove our human tapestry."

Pete continued his tireless work on civil rights, peace movements, and environmental issues, including the cleanup of the Hudson River, with particular concern for that cause. As an individual performer, before his world tour in June 1963, Pete organised a concert at Carnegie Hall to benefit the Highland Folk School in Tennessee. The state had revoked the school's charter, and Seeger, along with other supporters, organised the concert to raise funds and support for the school and its associated legal fees. The concert took place on June 8, 1963. The highlight of the concert was Pete's performance of the iconic song "We Shall Overcome."

Upon his return to America, Pete headed back to the recording studio. In January 1964, he recorded " Little Boxes ", written by Malvina Reynolds, which reached No. 1 on the hit parade. Peter Seeger returned to the radio, stage, and TV as a popular performer. For the next decade, Pete's passion for environmental conservation, as well as his advocacy for civil rights causes and his live concert tours, continued.

Show me the country where bombs had to fall,
Show me the ruins of buildings once so tall,
And I'll show you a young land with so many reasons why
There but for fortune, go you or go I -- you and I.
You and I,
There but for fortune, go you or go I -- you and I

" There but for fortune", Phil Ochs

CHAPTER 8.

BUILDING A DREAM

Pete was barely five years old when he had his first sailing experience. The family had taken a vacation near Long Island; he was strapped into a life jacket and told to sit on a seat at the back of the boat and not to move. Everyone else on board had jobs to do, from pulling ropes to trimming sails to steering and turning towards the aft, all while having loads of fun. He did not enjoy it at all, and he wasn't keen on sailing until around age forty. At the time, he had a job in Cape Cod, and a teenage boy took him out in the middle of the night in a small boat about ten feet long with just one sail. The boy taught him a bit about how to turn the vessel left and right, how to catch the wind in the sail to make it go fast or slow, and how to turn around again quickly. He realised it was a game of catching the wind and riding the **waves, and in that, he found something spiritual.**

Back on the Hudson near his home in Beacon, he bought a little plastic boat and taught himself to sail it. Tosh, his wife, had said, 'Are you okay to get out there on your own?' Pete's reply was, 'Not only am I okay, but I'm going to stay out on the river all night and enjoy it." It was like the poetry of a song to him, watching the sky change from bright blue to grey and dark, and the mountains shift from purple to black. The day transformed from golden to grey. It was awe-inspiring, and there he wrote songs.

He became interested in sailing and subsequently in Hudson River sloops — the traditional cargo-carrying sailing vessels of the Hudson River — and he got an idea. Perhaps we could build a ship that was so grand, so extraordinary, and one that had not sailed the river in a very long time. Maybe we could draw people down to the banks of a river that had long ago been forsaken. Pete saw potential where others did not, and believed in and visualised a ship that would ultimately be called Clearwater. He envisioned "Clearwater" as a vessel that could bring people to the river, have them sing songs, and perhaps help them "love their river again."

Pete Seeger's inspiration to build a Hudson River sloop came in 1963 when his mate, Vic Schwarz, lent him a copy of the 1908 book *Sloops of the Hudson*, written by William Verplanck and Moses Collyer, two retired sloop captains. He read it in a single night. Some time passed before Pete wrote his friend a five-page letter, which started: *"One way to see if a pipe dream has any practicality is to get it down on paper. So I'm writing to you now with the most grandiose and ambitious plan. It will make our wives groan. It will probably never get beyond the paper stage, but here goes:"* He wrote the letter and then forgot about it. It was September 1965. Vic, however, did not forget the letter and began chatting up fellow commuters on the train to New York. That fall, Vic called up Pete and asked, "When are we going to start building that sloop?" Pete answered, "You must be kidding!"

The challenges that the Clearwater organisation faced were numerous. First and foremost, perhaps, was the fact that it was the 1960s. The Vietnam War was raging and growing increasingly unpopular. So unpopular that President Lyndon B. Johnson declared in a nationally televised address in March 1968 that he would not run for re-election. The Rev. Martin Luther King Jr. was assassinated in April of that year, igniting riots in over 100 American cities. Robert Kennedy was assassinated in June. In

August, there were violent clashes between police and protesters in Chicago during the Democratic National Convention.

Much of what we know about how the rest of the story unfolded is due to the fact that, in the 1960s, people wrote letters and saved them. They also often saved carbon copies. Postage was inexpensive, but long-distance phone calls were not. After making a foray into the library at Mystic Seaport, Pete wrote a letter that December to Joel White, a boat designer and builder. Joel was the son of the writer E. B. White and had a boatyard in Brooklyn, Maine. White wrote back, telling Pete his shop was too small to build a boat that big, and he was too busy to do any design work. He did recommend naval architect Cyrus Hamlin of Southwest Harbour, Maine. "He is a fine architect, and I am sure you would like him," Joel wrote.

The following month -- January 1966 -- Pete and Vic met with Cyrus Hamlin at the National Boat Show in New York City. Pete and Cy hit it off. Cy sent a formal letter to Pete in February, outlining his estimate for the construction cost and a quotation for his design fee based on the forecast. In April, Pete wrote Cy a $500 personal check to cover the naval architect's "advance research" on the Hudson River sloop.

Pete's initial vision, as outlined in his letter to Vic, was for the sloop to be something like a floating timeshare. Off the top of his head, he estimated that a 55-foot sloop might cost $100,000 to build. That was more money than he and Vic could scrape together, so he suggested that they try to form "Hudson River Sloop Clubs" up and down the river. If there were 10 clubs, then each would have to raise $10,000 to build the vessel, and each club could sail the sloop for a week at a time.

Eventually, as we know, a non-profit was formed. The Hudson River Sloop Restoration was incorporated in September 1966. Interestingly, nowhere in the Articles of Incorporation is there any mention of the organisation having an environmental purpose. Instead, the document states the purpose as:
"To acquaint people with matters relating to our cultural heritage; and to maintain and promote interest in the history of the Hudson River both as a commercial and pleasure artery; and in connection therewith to build, own, operate and exhibit replicas of the great sloops which once freely navigated the river, thereby generating a greater interest in our cultural heritage and an understanding of the contributions made to our culture and commerce by the river and the sloops which sailed it."

Determining whether the sloop could be classified as a "yacht" or would need to be classified as a "passenger-carrying vessel," thus making it subject to United States Coast Guard regulations and inspection, was an important decision that had to be made. Complying with USCG regulations would increase the sloop's building and operating costs. It would also mean that it could not serve as a historically accurate replica, and perhaps not even be particularly visually appealing. At issue was the tragic sinking of the brigantine "Albatross" in 1961. A "school ship" carrying 13 American teenagers and five crew members sank in a sudden squall in the Gulf of Mexico. Six lives were lost, including four of the students. Although the ship was Panamanian registered, the USCG investigated the accident. Further analysis led to the publication of On the Stability of Sailing Vessels by USCG officers

John G. Beebe-Centre and Richard B. Brooks in 1966. This work questioned the reliability of traditional stability assessment techniques for sailing vessels and resulted in the adoption of more stringent US Coast Guard (USCG) stability criteria.

Cy retained a Boston-based attorney in the spring of 1966 on behalf of Pete and the "sloop committee" to help facilitate a dialogue with the Coast Guard and explore various possibilities for the future vessel's operation. One option that was examined was to form a cooperative, wherein all the members of the cooperative would be considered "shareholders" and thereby owners of the vessel.

Ultimately, Cy convinced HRSR to build their sloop to meet Coast Guard regulations, likely the first sailing vessel built to meet the new, more stringent stability requirements. This was not until as late as May or June 1968, and there was still no plan to carry paying passengers. When exactly Pete realised that the sloop could be a tool to help clean up the river, we don't know. However, in a New York Times article written following the organisation's first major fundraiser on October 2, 1966, he's quoted as follows:

"Some people might think it's the most frivolous thing in the world to raise money for a sailboat." But we want people to love the Hudson, not think of it as a convenient sewer."

Despite Pete's "green" inclinations, it was clear that many people within the organisation were solely interested in maritime history and had no interest in being standard-bearers for the environmental movement. This is reflected in the results of a membership vote held in March 1969 to name the sloop. There were 44 names nominated. Some of them were pretty silly, such as "Greasy Luck" and "Sewer Rat" In the end, the name 'Clearwater' narrowly edged out on "Heritage " with "Hope for the Hudson", placing third.

While there may not have been existing Hudson River sloops for Cy to study, he was able to research the vessel through builders' half-hull models, periodicals and reference works, including John W. Griffith's Treatise on Marine and Naval Architecture, published in 1850, and Lauchlan McKay's The Practical Shipbuilder, published in 1839. He gleaned information about rigging details through paintings, period photographs and even a placemat or two that he discovered in a gift shop. He also had access to photos and drawings from Howard Chapelle, the great American naval architect and maritime historian, who was then a senior historian at the Smithsonian Institution. "Chap" provided Cy with the lines of the 1848 sloop "Victorian " and two others. Ultimately, Pete and company decided their sloop should measure approximately 75 feet long, as this would allow for more headroom below decks. Cy presented preliminary drawings at the organisation's annual membership meeting on November 5, 1967.

By late January of 1968, Cy had performed the necessary work to put the sloop project out to bid. He sent bidding documents to at least three yards in Maine and three in New York, including Rondout Marine. Cy also inquired with at least two yards overseas – one in Spain and another in Yugoslavia – where he had connections. Soliciting a bid from a foreign yard was not his idea. The organisation thought that a foreign-built vessel might be less expensive. So Cy also agreed to look into shipyards in Nova Scotia. It was his opinion, however, that "the desirability of a yard is probably inversely proportional to the distance from the United States."

In the end, Harvey F. Gamage, Shipbuilder, Inc. of South Bristol, Maine, submitted the lowest bid among the yards that submitted bids — there is no evidence that any foreign yard did — and was awarded the contract. Construction of the sloop began in August 1968. There was a keel-laying ceremony at the shipyard on October 18, attended by about 50 HRSR members. Toshi Seeger anointed the length of the sloop's keel with Hudson River water, and Pete led everyone in song. After two years of recruiting new members and vigorous fundraising, there was finally something concrete to celebrate. Over the next several months, however, a lot more money still needed to be raised. Approximately 200 guests attended a special fundraiser hosted by Mr. & Mrs. Steven Rockefeller at the Rockefeller Farm Barn at Pocantico Hills in November. There were informational meetings and slide show presentations at Rotary clubs, libraries, and coffeehouses. Numerous concerts were held, including a sold-out performance at Carnegie Hall in April 1969. On May 17, a crowd of about 2,500 gathered at the shipyard. People packed inside the boat shed to hear speeches and celebrate the occasion with a song. At approximately 12:30 PM -- high tide -- Clearwater slid down the marine railway and into the waters of a quiet cove alongside the Damariscotta River. The schooner "Bowdoin" was in attendance, as was Maine's governor, Kenneth Curtis. It was a belated birthday present for Pete, who had turned 50 precisely two weeks earlier.

Over the next six weeks, the ship's crew got busy rigging, fitting out, and provisioning the vessel. There were sea trials and Coast Guard inspections. But before the sloop could leave South Bristol, the shipbuilder needed to be paid in full. In the days before the sloop set sail, Toshi Seeger frantically called up several friends -- people she and Pete knew from the folk music world -- to secure personal loans to pay the bill. The Newport Folk Festival loaned the organisation $10,000. The Seegers contributed an additional $7,000.

Finally, on June 27, the sloop set sail for Portland, the first stop on its journey. One of the plans to raise money was to give a series of concerts at various ports-of-call between Maine and New York on the sloop's maiden voyage. To this end, most of the sailing crew consisted of Pete's musician friends. Billed as the "Hudson River Sloop Singers," the group included Pete, Capt. Allan Aunapu, Louis Killen, Gordon Bok, Don McLean, Jimmy Collier, Rev. Frederick Douglass Kirkpatrick, Ramblin' Jack Elliott and others. They made about 20 appearances, including at The Fens in Boston and the Newport Folk Festival. The money raised made it possible to begin to repay those loans.

On August 1, 1969, "Clearwater" tied up at the South Street Seaport to much fanfare, with New York City Mayor John Lindsay onboard. What had started as a "pipe dream" nearly four years earlier was now a reality. A Hudson River sloop would be sailing the river once again. Fifty years later, "Clearwater" is still sailing. From onboard, hundreds of thousands of schoolchildren -- and group sail participants of all ages -- have experienced the beauty and wonder of the Hudson River ecosystem. Clearwater's award-winning education program has provided a model for organisations around the country, and the sloop remains a powerful symbol in the fight for clean water and a healthier, greener planet.

Sailing down my golden river,

Sailing down my golden river
Sun and water all my own
Yet I was never alone

Sun and water, old life givers
I'll have them wherever I roam
And I was not far from home
Sunlight glancing on the water

Life and death are all my own
Yet I was never alone
… Life for all my sons and daughters
Golden sparkles in the foam
And I was not far from home

Sailing down this winding highway
Travellers from near and far
And I was never alone
Exploring all the little byways.

Sighting all the distant stars
And I was not far from home
Sailing down my golden river
Sun and water all my own
Yet I was never alone

Sun and water, old life givers
I'll have them wherever I roam
And I was not far from home
… Yet I was never alone
And I was not far from home

Lyrics & Music—Pete Seeger

Sailing down my dirty stream

Sailing down my murky stream,
still I love it, and I'll keep the dream
that one day, perhaps not this year,
my Hudson River will run clear once more.

It starts high in the mountains of the north,
Crystal clear and icy, trickles forth
with just a few floating wrappers of chewing gum
dropped by some hikers to warn of things to come.

At Glens Falls, five thousand honest hands
work at the consolidated paper plant
. Five million gallons of waste a day
. Why should we do it any other way?

Down the valley, one million toilet chains
Find my Hudson so convenient a place to drain
And each little city says, "Who, me?
Do you think that sewage plants come free?"

Out in the ocean, they say the water's clear, but I live right here at
Beacon, way between the mountains and the sea, tacking to and
fro, this thought keeps returning to me.

Well, I'm sailing up my dirty stream.
Still, I love it, and I'll dream that one day,
although perhaps not this year,
my Hudson and my country will run clear.

CHAPTER 9

MY COUNTRY AFTER ALL

Always the activist for cleaning up the Hudson, Peter and fellow folk musicians held many concerts along the Hudson River and on board the Clearwater in the mid-to-late 1960s. He never gave up on peace movements either. As a longstanding opponent of the arms race and of the Vietnam War, Seeger satirically attacked then-President Lyndon Johnson with his 1966 recording, on the album Dangerous Songs of Len Chandler's children's song " Beans in my Ears" Beyond Chandler's lyrics, Seeger said that "Mrs. Jay's little son Alby" had "beans in his ears", implying that "Alby Jay" (a loose pronunciation of Johnson's nickname "LBJ") was deaf to war protesters' concerns.

During 1966, Seeger and Malvina Reynolds participated in environmental activism. The album "God Bless the Grass" was released in January of that year and became the first album in history to be wholly dedicated to songs about environmental issues. The same ideologies informed their politics of nationalism, populism, and criticism of big business.

Seeger attracted wider attention starting in 1967 with his song " Waist Deep in the Big Muddy "about a captain, referred to in the lyrics as "the big fool", who drowned while leading a platoon on manoeuvres in Louisiana during World War II. With its lyrics about a platoon being led into danger by an ignorant captain, the song's anti-war message was obvious—the line "the big fool said to push on" is repeated several times. In the face of arguments with the management of CBS about whether the song's political weight was in keeping with the usually light-hearted entertainment of the Smothers Brothers Comedy Hour, the final lines were "Every time I read the paper/those old feelings come on/We are waist deep in the Big Muddy and the big fool says to push on." The lyrics could be interpreted as an allegory of Johnson as the "big fool" and the Vietnam War as the foreseeable danger. Although the performance was cut from the September 1967 show, after wide publicity, it was broadcast when Seeger appeared again on the Smothers' Brothers show on February 25, 1968

Peter had recorded eight albums of his songs over his lifetime. In April 1971, Pete entered the recording studio with fellow folk musicians to record his Rainbow Race album for Columbia. He had achieved so much as an environmentalist, peacemaker, protector, folk singer, and political activist that it seemed natural for this album to celebrate its strong focus on social issues and its contemporary sounds of that time. Reviewers praised it for its powerful protest songs, particularly the five live tracks recorded at 1960s concerts during the era of protest. It was highlighted as an example of Pete Seeger's work, blending his traditional folk style with something more modern. Perhaps it was the influence of artists like Bob Dylan, Phil Ochs, and Joan Baez that steered him in that direction, but it was undoubtedly an album relevant to the time. The album is noted for its contemporary sound, which some reviewers found interesting compared to Seeger's more traditional folk music. One reviewer calls out the song "Bring Them Home" as a "tour de force."

The album is generally well-received, with many reviewers suggesting it's a great introduction to Seeger's work for younger listeners and a worthwhile revisit for those familiar with his music. The "Rainbow Race" is celebrated for its strong folk songs that address social issues and its contemporary sound for the time. Reviewers praise its powerful protest songs, particularly those from the live tracks, and appreciate its reflection of the 1960s protest era. The album is considered a great example of Pete Seeger's work, blending his traditional folk style with a more modern approach. Perhaps it was the rise of Bob Dylan, Phil Ochs, and Joan Baez at the time—fundamental protest singers of the age who also influenced Pete.

In 1980, the Weavers reunited for a concert that was recorded and released as a live album. This reunion followed the group's disbandment and helped to boost their popularity once more. The quartet performed two final concerts at Carnegie Hall on November 28th and 29th, 1980. These performances marked a significant reunion for the group and were their last full concerts together. The concerts commemorated the 25th anniversary of their first reunion and drew considerable anticipation, with some considering them more desired than a Beatles reunion. The concerts featured many of the Weavers' classic songs such as "Good Night Irene," "Kisses sweeter than wine," and "Wimoweh." The event also included international songs, such as "Venga Jaleo," reflecting the group's political background. These performances were recorded and later released as the album "Together Again."

In 1980, Carnegie Hall concerts were a poignant moment for the Weavers, particularly as they were one of the final performances for Lee Hays, who was ill and using a wheelchair at the time. The group did have one final informal "rehearsal" at the Clearwater Festival in June 1981, but the 1980 Carnegie Hall concerts were their last full public performances.

In December 1994, Pete Seeger received the highest award given to artists by the U.S. government. He also received the Kennedy Centre Honours that same year. The suits he wore belonged to his father, who had worn them since 1922, which had been let out a few inches for Pete. He had never needed a suit before, but conceded on this occasion and felt some pride in wearing his father's suit to receive the award. The Kennedy Centre Honours were presented by President Clinton, who called him "an inconvenient artist who dared to sing things as he saw them." (The Kennedy Centre Honours recognise lifetime achievement in the performing arts.) Pete must have found it a bit ironic that only a few decades earlier, he was considered a communist, while everyone around him was anti-government. And here, with the same political party, a modern-day president is giving him two awards in one year. It must have seemed to Pete that the government wanted to make amends for past errors. It takes a humble man to let go of the pain and strife that Pete and his family experienced during the McCarthy era and the years of unemployment due to the media bias against folk with non-conservative views.

Pete Seeger appears in the 1997 documentary film "An Act of Conscience", which was filmed between 1988 and 1995. In the movie, Seeger joins a group of demonstrators protesting in support of the war tax resistance movement and Andy Kehler and Betsy Corner, whose home was seized by the Internal Revenue Service (IRS) after the couple openly refused to pay their federal income taxes as a protest against war and military spending. Then, in September 2003

Pete Seeger participated in an anti-war protest against the Iraq War. Suppose there was a course for the betterment of people. Pete was always up front and centre.

On March 16, 2007, Pete Seeger, his sister Peggy, his brothers Mike and John, his wife Toshi, and other family members spoke and performed at a symposium and concert sponsored by the American Folklife Centre in honour of the Seeger family, held at the Library of Congress in Washington D.C, where Pete had been employed by the Archive of American Folk Song 67 years earlier.

In September 2008, Pete Seeger released the album "At 89," which won the Grammy Award for Best Traditional Folk Album, released by Appleseed Recordings. This was Seeger's second Grammy win in this category, as his 1996 CD "Pete" had also won the same award. The release of "At 89" was significant, featuring Seeger in a rare national TV appearance on the "Late Show with David Letterman" to promote it. On January 18, 2002, Pete and his grandson Tao Rodriguez Seeger joined Bruce Springsteen and the audience in singing Woody Guthrie's "This Land Is Your Land" during the finale of Barack Obama's inaugural concert in Washington, D.C. The performance was noteworthy for including two verses not often featured in the song: one about a 'private property' sign, which the narrator cheerfully ignores, and another making a passing reference to the Depression-era relief office. The final line of the former, however, "This land was made for you and me," is modified to "This side was made for you and me." Over the years, he lent his fame to support numerous environmental organisations, including South Jersey's Bayshore Centre, home to New Jersey's tall ship, the oyster schooner *A.J. Meerwald*. Seeger's benefit concerts helped raise funds for various groups, enabling them to continue educating and spreading environmental awareness. On May 3, 2009, at the Clearwater Concert, dozens of musicians gathered in New York at Madison Square Garden to celebrate Seeger's 90th birthday, which was later televised on PBS during the summer.

On October 21, 2011, at age 92, Pete Seeger was part of a solidarity march with Occupy Wall Street to Columbus Circle in New York CityThe march began with Seeger and fellow musicians exiting Symphony Space (95th and Broadway), where they had performed as part of a benefit for Seeger's Clearwater organisation. Thousands of people crowded around Pete Seeger by the time they reached Columbus Circle, where he performed with his grandson, Teo, Arlo Guthrie, David Amram, and other celebrated musicians. The event, promoted under the name OccupyTheCircle, was live-streamed and was dubbed by some "the Pete Seeger March".

In January 2012, Seeger joined the Rivertown Kids to pay tribute to his friend Bob Dylan, performing Dylan's "Forever Young" on the Amnesty International album Chimes of Freedom. This song, Seeger's last single, also marked his only music video, which went viral in the wake of his death two years later.

On December 14, 2012, Seeger performed alongside Harry Belafonte, Jackson Browne, Common, and others at a concert aimed at raising awareness of the 37-year-long plight of Native American activist Leonard Peltier. The concert took place at the Beacon Theatre in New York City. One of the organisers said, at the time. "Pete would want us to gather together and make some music." Many singers were invited to appear, but his visa was not approved in time by the United States government. In line with

Seeger's long-standing advocacy for environmental issues, the proceeds from the event supported the Hudson River sloop Clearwater, a nonprofit organisation founded by Seeger in 1966 to protect and restore the Hudson River. Seeger's 90th birthday was also celebrated at The College of Staten Island on May 4. On September 19, 2009, Seeger made his first appearance at the 52nd Monterey Jazz Festival, a notable event as the festival typically does not feature folk artists.

In 2010, still active at the age of 91, Seeger co-wrote and performed the song "God's Counting on Me, God's Counting on You.". A performance of the song by Seeger, Wyatt, and friends was recorded and filmed aboard the sloop *Clearwater* in August for a single and video produced by Richard Barone and Matthew Billy, released on election day, November 6, 2012. On August 9, 2013, one month after becoming a widower, Seeger was in New York City for the 400-year commemoration of the Two Row Wampum Tribe between the Iroquois and the Dutch. In an interview he gave that day to Democracy Now, Seeger sang "I Come and Stand at Every Door", as it was also the 68th anniversary of the bombing of Nagasaki.

On September 21, 2013, Seeger performed at Farm Aid at the Saratoga Performing Arts Centre in New York. Joined by Willie Nelson, Neil Young, John Mellencamp, and Dave Matthews, he sang "This Land Is Your Land" and included a verse he said he had written specifically for the Farm Aid concert. On July 9, 2013, Toshi Seeger passed away. She was 91 at the time. Pete died six months later, on January 27, 2014, at age 94, back in New York.
The power of song, as he constantly reminded us, can take us through everything life and death throw our way. On February

22nd, we won't take a moment of silence to remember him. Instead, we will take all the moments to sing – as loudly and with as many harmonies as we can muster. If Pete heard we were going to honour him by not singing, he would be furious! If you love Pete, how can you keep from singing!" - Nora Guthrie, daughter of Woody Guthrie

Eleven years ago, on February 22, 2014, the Tulsa-based Woody Guthrie Centre and the Los Angeles-based Grammy Museum celebrated the late Pete Seeger with the inaugural Woody Guthrie Prize at the Peter Norton Symphony Space in New York City. The event and award presentation marked a tribute to Pete Seeger's musical legacy, as well as his connection to Woody Guthrie and his work. Pete was meant to accept the award and perform at the event before his passing on January 27th.

The Woody Guthrie Prize is given annually to the artist who best exemplifies the spirit and life's work of Woody Guthrie by speaking for the less fortunate through music, film, literature, dance or other art forms and serving as a positive force for social change in America. Proceeds from the event supported the Woody Guthrie Centre, a 12,000-square-foot centre featuring state-of-the-art, interactive exhibits on Woody Guthrie's life, art, and creative legacy. The centre is home to Woody's comprehensive archives, including the original, handwritten version of his landmark anthem, "This Land is Your Land".Pete had been thrilled to be included in this fundraiser for the newly established Woody Guthrie Centre in Tulsa, Oklahoma. As the first recipient of the Woody Guthrie Prize, there can be no better person to set the standard than Pete. He was always available for a worthy cause. As his wife of 70 years, Toshi joked, 'I would have left him years ago, if only it were for another woman. Unfortunately, he was always away for another 'cause!' It's up to us now to step in and make sure all the 'causes' that Pete believed in get our support."

Pete Seeger has always walked the road less travelled. A tall, lean fellow with long arms and legs, high energy and a contagious joy of spirit, he set everything in motion, singing in that magical voice, his head thrown back as though calling to the heavens, making you see that you can change the world, risk everything, do your best, cast away stones. "Bells of Rhymney, "Where Have All the Flowers Gone?" "One Grain of Sand," "Oh, Had I a Golden Thread" -songs scattered along our path like jewels, from the present into the past, and back, along the road to the future. - Arlo Guthrie

Many folk singers write songs about current events, and Pete Seeger was no different. "We Shall Overcome", which he co-wrote, was a song often sung during civil rights protests of the 1960s. "Turn! Turn! Turn!", a song popularised by the Byrds in 1965, draws its lyrics from the Bible's Book of Ecclesiastes. It states that there is a time and a place for everything - even war. The song was released during the height of the Vietnam War. Its last line is "A time for peace, I swear it's not too late." In April 2000, Pete Seeger was recognised during the yearlong celebration of the Bicentennial. The Library of Congress recognises several Americans whose varied creative contributions to American life have made them living legends, and Pete Seeger was named among them.

It's worth repeating this when considering Pete's views on life and belief: "Nobody knows for sure. But people undoubtedly get feelings which are not explainable, and they feel they're talking to

God or they're talking to their parents who are long dead. I feel most spiritual when I'm out in the woods. I feel part of nature. Or looking up at the stars. [I used to say] I was an atheist. Now I say it's all according to your definition of God. According to my definition of God, I'm not an atheist. Because I think God is everything. Whenever I open my eyes, I'm looking at God. Whenever I'm listening to something, I'm listening to God. I've had preachers of the gospel, Presbyterians and Methodists saying, "Pete, I feel that you are a very spiritual person." And maybe I am. I feel strongly that I'm trying to raise people's spirits to get together. ... I tell people I don't think God is an old white man with a long white beard and no navel; nor do I believe God is an old black woman with white hair and no navel. However, I believe God is everything because I don't think something can come from nothing. And so, there has always been something. It's always a long time.

I am glad I grew up listening to Pete Seeger and The Weavers' folk music. I was privileged to attend a Pete Seeger concert, to listen to his music during my young, impressionable years, and to watch many documentaries about this remarkable human being. Pete Seeger contributed more to humanity in the ninety-four years he spent on this earth than most people can claim. He exemplified what we are all supposed to do: use our talent—be it one, five, or ten—for the betterment of humanity and the earth we inhabit. I now trust that the template of Pete Seeger's life and work remains a beacon to guide us forward on this ongoing journey for all of us.

CHAPTER 10

EPILOGUE

It would be remiss of me not to include a few song lyrics from the many songs Pete penned and sang over his lifetime, with my unapproved licence to include some interpretations from my viewpoint.

"Little Boxes" was written by Malvina Reynolds as a critique of suburban life and the perceived lack of individuality it often entails. Pete Seeger's recording and performance of the song in 1963 helped popularise it as an influential piece of the folk and protest music movement. The lyrics describe suburban houses as "little boxes" that are all the same, built with "ticky-tacky" materials, and inhabited by people who fit into predetermined roles. "Little Boxes" became a symbol of social commentary and a critique of the prevailing cultural trends of the time.

Little boxes on the hillside
Little boxes made of ticky-tacky
Little boxes on the hillside
Little boxes all the same

There's a green one,
a pink one, a blue one, and a yellow one.
They're all made from ticky-tacky
and look just the same.

And the people in the houses all went to university,
where they were placed in boxes and came out all the same.

And there are doctors and lawyers
and business executives
, and they're all made out of ticky-tacky
and they all look just the same.

And they all play on the golf course
and drink their martinis dry.
And they all have lovely children,
and the children go to school.
And the children go to summer camp,
and then to university,
where they are placed in boxes,
and they come out all the same.

And the boys go into business.
And marry and raise a family.
In boxes made of ticky-tacky,
and they all look just the same.

There's a pink one and a green one,
and a blue one and a yellow one.
And they're all made out of ticky-tacky,
And they all look just the same.

Where Have All the Flowers Gone?   Pete Seeger wrote the first three verses in 1955, drawing inspiration from the traditional Cossack song "Koloda-Duda".   The song follows a circular structure, with verses that repeat and build upon each other, creating a sense of inevitability. It explores themes of loss, the impact of war, and the passage of time, using the imagery of flowers, girls, husbands, soldiers, and graveyards.

The song was further developed by Joe Hickerson in 1960 and has been covered by many artists, including The Kingston Trio and Marlene Dietrich, who performed it in multiple languages. The song's message of peace and reflection on the consequences of conflict resonated deeply, particularly in the aftermath of World War II. "Where Have All the Flowers Gone?" has been recognised as a powerful anti-war song, demonstrating the enduring impact of folk music in conveying social and political messages

Where have all the flowers gone
Long time passing
Where have all the flowers gone
A long time ago

Where have all the flowers gone
Young girls have picked them everyone
Oh, when will you ever learn
Oh, when will you ever learn

Where have all the young girls gone
Long time passing
Where have all the young girls gone
long time ago

Where have all the young girls gone
They've taken husbands every one
Oh, when will you ever learn
Oh, when will you ever learn

Where have all the young men gone
Long time passing
Where have all the young men gone
long time ago

Where have all the young men gone
They're all in uniform
Oh, when will we ever learn
Oh, when will we ever learn?

Joe Hickerson, a mate of Seeger's, added two more verses in 1960, including the "graveyards" and "flowers" verse, transforming it into a cyclical song. Seeger acknowledged Hickerson's contribution and even gave him 20% of the royalties.

Where have all the soldiers gone?
long time passing
Where have all the soldiers gone
long time ago.

Where have all the soldiers gone?
They've gone to the graveyard, everyone.
When will they ever learn?
When will they ever learn

Where have all the graveyards gone?
long time passing,
Where have all the graveyards gone
A long time ago,
where have all the graveyards gone?
They've gone to flowers, everyone.

Where have all the flowers gone
Young girls have picked them, everyone
When will they ever learn
When will they ever learn

Turn! Turn! (To Everything There is a Season)," A song written by Pete Seeger in the late 1950s takes its lyrics from the third chapter of Ecclesiastes in the King James Version (1611) of the Bible. The Byrds, an American folk rock band, immortalised the song in 1965.

To everything (Turn, turn, turn)
There is a season (Turn, turn, turn)
And a time for every purpose under heaven

A time to be born, a time to die
A time to plant, a time to reap
A time to kill, a time to heal
A time to laugh, a time to weep

To everything (Turn, turn, turn)
There is a season (Turn, turn, turn)
And a time for every purpose under heaven

A time to build up, a time to break down
A time to dance, a time to mourn
A time to cast away stones

A time to gather stones together

To everything (Turn, turn, turn)
There is a season (Turn, turn, turn)
And a time for every purpose under heaven

A time of love, a time of hate
A time of war, a time of peace
A time you may embrace
A time to refrain from embracing

To everything (Turn, turn, turn)
There is a season (Turn, turn, turn)
And a time to every purpose under heaven

A time to gain, a time to lose
A time to rend, a time to sew
A time of love, a time of hate
A time of peace, I swear it's not too late

To everything (Turn, turn, turn)
There is a season (Turn, turn, turn)
And a time to every purpose under heaven
To everything (Turn, turn, turn)
There is a season (Turn, turn, turn)
And a time to every purpose under heaven.

"If I Had a Hammer" was written by Pete Seeger and Lee Hays in 1949 as an anthem for many progressive concerns of the day, particularly the Labour Movement. The song features images of blue-collar workers (hammers and bells to suggest factories, etc.)

as a rallying call for justice and equality, a message that still resonates today. Pete Seeger wrote back then, *"Dear fellow human beings: humanity doesn't have another 2000 years to learn to love their neighbour. We must change the conditions of our life so love flows from it, and good humour flows from it as it would from a happy family. Let us open our eyes and ears to one another. Let's exchange messages with each other back and forth. And so I'm here tonight; the most I can do is sing you some of the songs I know. Then Peter began with this one."*

If I had a hammer, I'd hammer in the morning. I'd hammer in the evening, all over this land.

 I'd hammer out danger, I'd hammer out a warning. I'd hammer out love between my brothers and my sisters, all over this land, ooh.

If I had a bell, I'd ring it in the morning. I'd ring it in the evening all over this land.

 I'd ring out danger, I'd ring out a warning. I'd ring out love between my brothers and my sisters, all over this land, ooh.

If I had a song, I'd sing it in the morning. I'd sing it in the evening all over this land

. I'd sing out danger, I'd sing out a warning. I'd sing out love between my brothers and my sisters all over this land, ooh.

Well, I've got a hammer, and I've got a bell. I've got a song to sing across this land.

It's the hammer of justice; it's the bell of freedom. It's a song about love among my brothers and sisters all over this land.

It's the hammer of justice. It's the bell of freedom. It's a song about love between my brothers and sisters all over this land.

Pete Seeger's arguably most influential song was "We Shall Overcome." While not originally written by him, he played a crucial role in popularising it as the anthem of the Civil Rights movement. Seeger adapted the song from a 19th-century African-American gospel piece and introduced it to a broader audience, including Martin Luther King Jr. He also famously performed it at Carnegie Hall in 1963 and at his 90th birthday concert.

"We Shall Overcome" is considered one of the most influential anthems of the Civil Rights movement. The song became a symbol of hope and perseverance for activists fighting for racial equality. Seeger's version, with his slight lyrical change from "We will overcome " to "We shall overcome," is the version that is widely recognised today. The song's simple yet powerful message resonated deeply with those facing adversity and injustice, making it a powerful tool for social change. "We Shall Overcome" continues to be sung at protests and rallies for social justice around the world, a testament to its enduring influence.

The song has had a lasting effect on my conscience, instilling heartfelt thanks and praise, for it resonates with the feeling of the loss of my son Peter, at his hand back in 2003. It was ten years later, as I stood at the base of a pile of rocks at Cruz Ferro, a Christian symbol above it with a crucifix, located at the highest point of the Camino de Santiago Way. This was once a pagan site—a mountain of stones, left behind by pilgrims who symbolically let go of their burdens by leaving a rock. I lay down a rock to with my sons date of birth written upon it in black texta- he was still alive in my heart...and then I heard a group of pilgrims standing on the mountain of rock, below the crucifix erected high up on a pole singing " We shall Overcome " Ans I knew that I would too.

So I think it is fitting to end this book with this song, for it is the template of many of Pete Seeger's songs that I still carry, and this book could go on forever. However, I leave it to you, the reader, to turn to Spotify or YouTube to hear more of Pete Seeger's songs if you are so inclined. Perhaps you will find, in time, a temple of one of his songs that resonates with your own heart's desires, too.

We shall overcome
We shall overcome
We shall overcome, someday.

Oh, deep in my heart
I do believe
We shall overcome, someday

We'll walk hand in hand.
We'll walk hand in hand.
We'll walk hand in hand.
We'll walk hand in hand, someday.

Deep in my heart
Oh, deep in my heart
I do believe
I do believe

We shall overcome, someday
We shall overcome, someday

We shall live in peace.
We shall live in peace
We shall live in peace someday.
We shall live in peace someday.

Oh, deep in my heart
I do believe
We shall overcome, someday

We are not afraid
We are not afraid
We are not scared, today
, Oh, deep in my heart
I do believe
We shall overcome, someday
We shall overcome, someday

The whole wide world around
The whole wide world around
The whole wide world around
The whole wide world around, someday

Oh, deep in my heart
I do believe
We shall overcome, someday
We shall overcome someday.

About the Author.

Doug McPhillips, poet, singer, songwriter, and author, commenced his journey of discovery over a decade ago after life-changing experiences.

The many tracks he has traversed through the Northern Hemisphere and down under in Australia and New Zealand have resulted s.in the facts and fiction of this novel.

Doug has sung songs related to his many works with majestic melodies in an authentic Australian style. Doug has recorded and

Doug has written several novels, two books of poems, a travel guide and three albums of his songs, all inspired by his adventures.

Doug is an adventurer who divides his time between family and friends, his creative pursuits, and those who benefit most from his efforts and experience.

22/6/25

www.ingramcontent.com/pod-product-compliance
Lightning Source LLC
Chambersburg PA
CBHW061210070526
44583CB00025B/3184